THE ROYAL HORTICULTURAL SOCIETY
PRACTICAL GUIDES

FLOWERING
SHRUBS

THE ROYAL HORTICULTURAL SOCIETY
PRACTICAL GUIDES

FLOWERING
SHRUBS

CHARLES CHESSHIRE

DORLING KINDERSLEY
LONDON • NEW YORK • SYDNEY • MOSCOW
www.dk.com

LONDON, NEW YORK, MUNICH, MELBOURNE, DELHI

Series Editor Pamela Brown
Series Art Editor Stephen Josland
Art Editor Rachael Parfitt

Managing Editor Louise Abbott
Managing Art Editor Lee Griffiths

DTP Designer Matthew Greenfield

Picture Researcher Louise Thomas
Production Ruth Charlton, Mandy Innes

First published in Great Britain in 1999
Reprinted 2003
by Dorling Kindersley Limited,
80 Strand, London WC2R 0RL

A Penguin Company

A CIP catalogue for this book is available from the British Library.
ISBN 0 7513 48597

Reproduced by Colourscan, Singapore
Printed and bound by Star Standard Industries, Singapore

See our complete catalogue at
www.dk.com

CONTENTS

SHRUBS IN THE GARDEN

WHAT IS A SHRUB?

SHRUBS ARE BUSHY PLANTS whose stems become woody with age, enabling them to survive winter weather and grow and flower for many years. Their lifespan varies from a few years to many decades, but in a garden context they are valued for the lasting beauty that they bring to planting schemes. There are many shrubs with lovely foliage, but the majority of garden favourites are chosen chiefly for their flowering displays.

WHY SHRUBS FLOWER

Shrubs flower to reproduce themselves, the blooms attracting pollinating insects that enable them to set seed. Most bear male and female flowers on the same plant, either fertilizing themselves or each other as insects move from flower to flower. Rarely, as with skimmias, male and female flowers are borne on separate plants and you need to grow both for a good display, but even with these, plant breeding has produced types that flower well alone.

WHY CHOOSE SHRUBS?

- Long-lasting, bring structure and interest to plantings year after year.
- Huge range of sizes, habits, flower colour and foliage interest from which to choose.
- Low-maintenance compared to other plant groups; most stand up well to bad weather.
- No nurturing of young plants or raising from seed is necessary.
- Flowering and fruiting shrubs attract wildlife, providing food and nesting sites.

EASY-CARE DISPLAYS
From the earliest flowers on bare spring branches, as with forsythia (left), to the richness of summer blooms such as buddleja (far left) and hibiscus (facing page), flowering shrubs bring colour and beauty to the garden through the seasons. Many, including the ones pictured here, are easy to grow and, once established, virtually look after themselves; some, such as the hibiscus, do not even need annual pruning.

BUDDLEJA DAVIDII 'FASCINATING'   *FORSYTHIA* 'ARNOLD GIANT'

◄ *HIBISCUS SYRIACUS* 'BLUE BIRD' *A showy shrub for full sun that flowers in late summer.*

SHRUBS IN PLANTING PLANS

It would be a poor garden that did not include any flowering shrubs. They have become increasingly popular because, in general, they require less maintenance than herbaceous plants, which die down in winter, and bedding, which must be regularly renewed, and form a backbone to planting schemes that persists year-round, important in the present day when gardens are smaller and planting schemes are more constantly in view. In fact, the traditional herbaceous border has largely disappeared

> It would be difficult to design a satisfying garden without shrubs

in favour of the "mixed" border, where shrubs and woody climbers lend height, structure and winter interest to plantings of annuals and perennials. Mixed borders may be planned to associate and contrast textures and colours across the different plant groups, or to give carefully paced

▲ SEASONAL CHEER
Shrubs (here a forsythia) add lasting, year-round interest near the house; even where there is no soil, many grow happily in tubs.

▼ FORM AND STRUCTURE
Berberis × stenophylla *makes an excellent hedge, but growing it as a specimen shrub, as here, lets it develop its lovely, arching habit.*

◄CITY CHOICE
As well as being good container plants, hydrangeas can also grow both in full sun and shade, and have a useful, long flowering season in late summer.

▼SETTING THE SCENE
Rhododendrons are perfect plants for acid soils under trees and in woodland areas, and associate naturally and beautifully with shade-loving perennials.

flowering displays throughout the year so that there is always something to admire, even in deepest winter.

Some flowering shrubs, like magnolias, can make spectacular specimen plants to be admired year-round, even for elegant bare branch structure, while others such as forsythia and spiraea, although having lovely flowers, have very dull foliage and form rather uninteresting mounds of greenery for the rest of the season; these are best merged with other shrubs and perennials that flower at different times.

Mass plantings of one kind of shrub can make for bold effects, and many can be useful for covering the ground, such as evergreen azaleas, cotoneasters, hebes, hypericums, viburnums and skimmias. This characteristic is often exploited for large public spaces but may be less appropriate for the small garden, since many of these plants are dull out of flower.

A number of flowering shrubs make fine hedges, adding colour, light and fragrance to boundaries. While many flower better grown informally, some, including thorny berberis and pyracantha, can be lightly clipped to form densely growing barriers.

YEAR-ROUND INTEREST

With careful planning, taking care to choose plants that are suited by the conditions your garden offers (climate, soil type, and sun or shade), you can have shrubs blooming year-round, with the scarcer autumn- and winter-flowerers supplemented by the glowing fruits and berries of many that flowered earlier in the season. Don't forget the value of foliage, too; fresh spring leaves, the rich autumn tints of some deciduous shrubs, and the year-round elegance of glossy evergreens.

THE FIRST FLOWERS

In late winter and very early spring, chimonanthus and hamamelis (witch hazel) carry flowers that are small, yet because they are borne on bare stems they show off to great advantage; moreover, both are intensely fragrant, and their scent may be enjoyed even before the shrub comes into view. Don't plant these shrubs too far away from the house, where they may not be visited in cold weather.

Both hamamelis and chimonanthus grow equally well in full sun or the shade of a woodland garden. Trees overhead will help, in cold climates, to protect early-flowering shrubs from damage by frost or cold wind. Such conditions, where the soil is acid, enable you to grow camellias, azaleas and rhododendrons, giving a wonderful display from early spring into early summer. Camellias and many rhododendrons have the advantage of being evergreen, providing a solid leafy background for their showy flowers. They could in turn be

---

Intense fragrance is a feature of many early-flowering shrubs

---

underplanted with heathers such as *Erica carnea*, which also flowers early. *Camellia × williamsii* hybrids may start flowering in mid-winter and continue into the spring, depending on the weather.

▲ *CHIMONANTHUS PRAECOX*
The small, waxy flowers of wintersweet are heavily fragrant, but the shrub needs a protected position.

▲ *CYTISUS* 'WINDLESHAM RUBY'
Cytisus are cheerful spring shrubs for full sun that grow fast but do not live long.

▲ *SYRINGA VULGARIS*
Lilacs (this is 'Sensation') are popular fragrant shrubs for late spring that need plenty of space to develop.

◄ SPRING FRESHNESS
*'The Bride' is one of
the finest exochordas.
It is compact and
spring-flowering, the
whole plant being
smothered in bloom.
It thrives in any soil
type, in full sun or in
partial shade.*

▼ SUMMER RICHNESS
*The deep purple
flowers of lespedeza
in late summer make
a good contrast
with* Hydrangea
paniculata *(see p.42).
It may be pruned
hard in late winter
to encourage these
long, vigorous
arching shoots.*

In more alkaline soils there are small, shrubby types of prunus which flower, in pink or white, on bare wood in early spring, such as *Prunus cerasifera* and *P.* × *cistena*, both of which have dark purple-leaved forms. *Chaenomeles* – the flowering quinces, or japonicas with bright red, pink and white flowers held tightly against the old wood look well growing as freestanding shrubs, up to 2.5m tall, or tied in and clipped flat against a wall. These and *Mahonia japonica* will grow in almost any soil, the latter bearing robust, fragrant spikes of yellow flowers above bold whorls of evergreen leaves.

Forsythia and flowering currants (*Ribes*) both flower at this time, looking delightful with an underplanting of early spring bulbs in bloom. Some people dislike forsythia for the very reason that others love it: its brilliant splash of yellow flowers, unalleviated by green leaves. The pungent, "catty" aroma of some ribes, especially *R. sanguineum*, can be a drawback.

THE START OF SUMMER

In late spring cytisus, ceanothus, exochorda and the heavily fragrant *Viburnum carlesii* and *V.* × *burkwoodii* will thrive in most soil types, and as summer begins, other fragrant shrubs like philadelphus and lilac begin flowering. Other fine shrubs for the turn of the seasons include kolkwitzia, deutzias, cistus, *Buddleja alternifolia* and escallonias, perhaps underplanted with helianthemums.

As the heat of summer arrives, low-growing hebes, hypericums and potentillas can fill in between larger shrubs. Shrubs that thrive in dry sites (*see pp.70–73*) are a boon in the summer garden, whatever the soil type. Hydrangeas are valuable at this time of year. The lacecaps are best for light shade, especially under trees, while the mophead hortensias are excellent container plants. The larger and very reliable *H. paniculata* has cones of white florets that fade to pink. It is best in full sun, where it would look good with abelias and

▲ LATE BLOOMERS
Grey-leaved shrubs that are hard-pruned in spring, like caryopteris ('Ferndown', above) and perovskia, reward the wait while their stems grow back through the summer with valuable late flowering displays.

◀ SECOND SHOW
Flowering shrubs that bear bright berries and fruits, like this cotoneaster, 'Exburyensis', double their value in the garden with a renewed season of interest in autumn.

lespedezas, with pink and purple flowers respectively. Two stalwarts for full sun are the butterfly bush, *Buddleja davidii* and its many varieties, and *Hibiscus syriacus*, both of which flower well into late summer. Perovskia and caryopteris are also ideal for the sunny garden, together with hardy fuchsias and lavender. In a warm year, late summer-bloomers will continue their show into autumn, when flowers become scarce. Other flowering shrubs may have new autumn attractions: the beautiful berries of cotoneaster and flame-coloured leaves of cotinus, for example.

PLANNING WITH COLOUR

It's not difficult to choose shrubs that will carry a colour theme year-round, or to vary the palette through the seasons to suit other plants (*see overleaf*) coming into bloom. Whites, pinks and yellows tend to predominate among spring-flowering shrubs, while richer, duskier hues are more the preserve of those that bloom in summer, but there are many exceptions to the rule. Shrubs with white flowers (*see below*) provide an attractive but neutral foil for almost any colour scheme.

MAHONIA × MEDIA 'CHARITY'
Some mahonias flower in autumn, others in spring. Autumn-bloomers such as 'Charity' can sometimes flower right through winter until spring-flowerers begin their display.

WHITE-FLOWERED SHRUBS

FOR WINTER-SPRING

Azaleas *Rhododendron* 'Palestrina' ♥ and 'Rose Greeley' are evergreen; 'Silver Slipper' ♥ is deciduous.
Camellias Look for *C. japonica* 'Alba Plena' or 'Mathotiana Alba', or for a smaller plant, perhaps for a tub, 'Cornish Snow' ♥.
***Chaenomeles speciosa* 'Nivalis'** Flowers on bare stems.
Daphne mezereum* f. *alba Fragrant.
Erica carnea Ground cover for acid soil; choose 'Springwood White' ♥ or 'Snow Queen'
***Exochorda* x *macrantha* 'The Bride'** ♥ May appear completely white when in full flower.
Rhododendron hybrids Evergreens for acid soil; 'Cunningham's White', 'Dora Amateis' ♥ , 'Loder's White' ♥ and 'Mrs P.D. Williams' ♥ are all tough and reliable.
Viburnums Many with the bonus of fragrance.

FOR SUMMER-AUTUMN

Deutzia gracilis Looks marvellous with roses.
***Escallonia* 'Iveyi'** ♥ Semi-evergreen, for warm gardens.
***Hydrangea paniculata, H. arborescens, H. quercifolia* ♥, *H. macrophylla* 'Lanarth White'** ♥ and 'Madame Emile Mouillière' ♥ Mainstays for the summer garden.
Hebe albicans ♥ Evergreen, for mild gardens.
***Hibiscus syriacus* 'Diana'** ♥ (*see p.41*)
***Lavandula angustifolia* 'Nana Alba'** A small lavender for fragrant edging.
Lilacs (*Syringa*) Large, fragrant flowerheads in many colours; 'Madame Lemoine' ♥, 'Mont Blanc' and 'Jan van Tol' are white.
Philadelphus Clusters of small flowers, intensely fragrant.
***Weigela* 'Candida'**.

SHRUBS WITH OTHER PLANTS

ALTHOUGH SHRUBS ARE VERY OFTEN grown together in groups known as shrubberies, it is often far more interesting to grow them in combination with other plants, mixing bulbs, herbaceous perennials, annuals and climbers among them. Equally, in a herbaceous planting, shrubs can be used to add height, weight and a longer season to what is often only a summer display.

UNDER- AND INTERPLANTING

Bulbs are perhaps the easiest of the other plant groups to add under shrub plantings because many can be left undisturbed and unattended for years. (This is the type of bulb planting known as "naturalized", as they will spread and form colonies of their own accord.) The bulbs often flower in the spring, benefiting from light before the leaves of the shrub have unfolded. As their foliage dies away, the burgeoning shrubs cover the unsightliness. Among herbaceous perennials, there are many that can cover ground beneath shrubs with the minimum of care: choose those that have attractive flowers and persistently attractive foliage. For the gaps between shrubs, you can choose low-maintenance perennials that complement the easy-care advantages of shrubs. Don't confine interplanting to low-growing plants: flower spikes and spires, such as foxgloves and verbascums, will add surprise vertical contrasts, and often self-seed to spring up randomly each year.

▲ SOFT COLOURS
This lavatera is flattered by Acer negundo *'Flamingo', a foliage shrub, and an underplanting of hardy perennial geraniums, a combination with a long season.*

▶ EXTROVERT PLANTING
The purple foliage of the cotinus is in dark contrast to the yellows of the genista behind and the red-hot poker (Kniphofia) *in the foreground: an adventurous scheme.*

◀ UNDERPLANTING
*In late winter,
snowdrops bloom in
the light that falls
between the flower-
studded bare branches
of* Hamamelis ×
intermedia *'Pallida'.*

▼ SHADY SCHEME
The pink buds of
Viburnum davidii
*break between
flowering euphorbias
and a background
of variegated holly
in this layered
planting design.*

CAREFUL COMBINATIONS

Some roses associate beautifully with other
flowering shrubs but require a little more
care: spring-flowering shrubs mix
brilliantly well with early wild roses, and as
the shrub rose season gets under way,
fragrant shrubs like philadelphus and lilac
produce a lovely, cottagey, summery feel.
There are climbers that can be allowed to
twine into shrubs as host supports; those
that die down in winter or are cut back in
spring will simplify pruning.

PLANT PARTNERS

Bulbs for underplanting: Woodland anemones
(*Anemone nemorosa, A. sylvestris*), scillas,
chionodoxas, narcissus (many small types
naturalize well), snowdrops (*Galanthus*).
Underplanting with a long season:
Aquilegias, astilbes, epimediums, ferns,
geraniums, hostas, persicarias and thalictrum.
Easy-care interplanting: Alchemillas, asters,
daylilies (*Hemerocallis*), iris, nepetas, peonies
and rudbeckias.
Vertical accents Foxgloves (*Digitalis*) and
lilies for shade, *Veronicastrum virginicum*
and verbascums for sun.
Climbers to scramble into shrubs: Clematis:
large-flowered hybrids, or the viticella types,
pruned hard in late winter; perennial peas
(*Lathyrus)* for large shrubs and sweet peas
for small ones; *Tropaeolum speciosum.*

SUITING THE SOIL

THERE ARE MANY SHRUBS that are remarkably unfussy as to the kinds of soil they enjoy, but there are also a number, including some very desirable plants, that have strict preferences. If these requirements are ignored, the shrubs will suffer, fail to grow and may even die. The primary considerations are for the texture, moisture and nutrient content of the soil, and for its acidity and alkalinity – known as its pH value.

STRUCTURE AND TEXTURE

Soil type ranges between two extremes, heavy clay and sand. Clay soil can be moulded in your hand when saturated with water, while sandy soil is light, dry and gritty-textured. If your soil seems to fall between these two types then you are fortunate: many shrubs will be happy in your garden. If it tends towards one extreme, choice will be more restricted.

Heavy clay soils have a naturally high level of nutrients but retain water, so avoid planting shrubs that like dry conditions. Plant roots take longer to penetrate clay, so lighten it by adding organic matter on planting. Ground that tends to become waterlogged at certain times of the year will kill many shrubs, especially evergreens. Some plants, such as amelanchier and clethra, tolerate and even enjoy occasional flooding. Sandy soils are easier to work but are free-draining and often low in nutrients, so add well-rotted manure as

> ## Waterlogging makes some shrubs die; others enjoy occasional flooding

well other organic matter, except for plants that prefer poor soils like cytisus, genista and tamarisk (*Tamarix*). In very poor soils full of builder's rubble, buddlejas thrive.

CHANGING COLOURS
If the soil is too limy, blue-flowered hydrangeas turn pink. On slightly limy soils they can be encouraged to retain their colour by adding aluminium sulphate and feeding well – but choosing other blue-flowered shrubs is a much easier option.

▲ *PIERIS* 'FOREST FLAME'
*Pieris belong to the same family as
rhododendrons and, like them, are ericaceous
plants, which means they prefer an acid soil.
This one has brilliant red young growth, and
carries clusters of white flowers in spring.*

◄ *PHILADELPHUS* 'BELLE ETOILE'
*A very reliable shrub with one of the strongest
perfumes of any plant. Philadelphus, or mock
orange, will grow on almost any soil, acid or
alkaline, that is fertile and well-drained.*

ACID OR ALKALINE?

The pH of your soil is easy to test with
simple kits available at most garden
centres. Plants that prefer acid soil are
often called "ericaceous" and include
rhododendrons and azaleas, pieris,
camellias, kalmia and ericas. If the pH is
too high for these plants, their leaves turn
yellow and they may die. It is difficult to
make an alkaline soil acid, so if you do
have chalky or limy soil it is best not to try
to grow this group of plants. However, if
you have slightly acid soil, you may find
that many of the plants that ideally prefer
chalky soils will grow perfectly well. Some
gardeners add garden lime to acid soil to
increase its pH for the benefit of plants
such as roses and Mediterranean shrubs,
like lavender and santolina.

CHALKY SOILS

Chalky soil does not pose nearly so many
problems as acid soil (see pp.56–59 for
suitable plants), but if your garden is on
chalk or limestone, try the following shrubs.
Many of them are equally happy in neutral
to acid soil.

Berberis	Tree peonies
Buddlejas	(*Paeonia delavayi,*
Cistus	*P. suffruticosa*)
Cotoneasters	Philadelphus
Hydrangea villosa	Potentillas
(not other species)	Prunus
Deutzias	Rosemary
Escallonias	(*Rosmarinus*)
Forsythias	Santolina
Kolkwitzia	*Sarcococca*
Lilac (*Syringa*)	Viburnums
Osmanthus	Weigelas

SUN AND SHADE

A N IMPORTANT FACTOR TO take into consideration before planting is what level of sun or shade a shrub prefers. This can also depend on the part of the world you are in. In northern Europe, where summers are relatively cool and the intensity of the sun is weak, many shade-loving plants are quite happy in full sun. Conversely, in regions where the summer sun is harsh and intense, many sun-loving shrubs may prefer to be, and grow happily in, some shade.

ASSESSING YOUR SITE

The degree of shade is crucial when choosing shrubs for your site. Deep shade (*see facing page*) is the most restrictive of choice, but part-day or light shade may deny you only the most committed sun-loving plants. However, although many shrubs will grow in shade, they may become shy of flowering. There are also different kinds of shade. The shade on the dark side of a building is deeper and more consistent than the shade cast by a tree. The shade under trees also varies, and affects the quality of the soil beneath.

> Dry soil can be an attribute of both sunny and shady sites

Camellias and rhododendrons will grow well under the dappled shade of deep-rooting oaks or sweet chestnuts, for instance, the annual leaf-fall enriching the soil to help them thrive, but shallow-rooting trees and conifers will not only shade the ground beneath but also deprive any shrubs of moisture and nutrition. Shrubs planted in such conditions may require additional irrigation and mulching with leafmould or compost.

Growing shrubs in full sun can also be variable. Buildings that are in full sun can reflect light and heat, especially if painted white, so that nearby plants with sensitive foliage will actually scorch in hotter climates. Plants grown on a south-facing bank not only receive a lot of light but also experience much more heat and dryness at the roots. In such harsh conditions there are plants such as abutilon, yucca, cytisus, grevillea, cistus and rosemary, native to dry regions such as Australia, South Africa or the Mediterranean, that would be ideal. In dry spells, these plants will still need watering until they are established.

YUCCA RECURVIFOLIA
Yucca is not only suitable for full sun but will also tolerate very dry situations, where it will be more likely to flower well. Yuccas provide a bold and striking accent in the border.

THE FOLIAGE FACTOR

Some variegated shrubs, especially shrubs with golden foliage such as *Philadelphus coronarius* 'Aureus' and *Sambucus racemosa* 'Sutherland Gold', whose parent species are happy in full sun, will burn in hot sun. The same plant, placed in deep shade, will lose its colour intensity. Getting light levels right lets you enjoy the full beauty of flower and foliage contrasts.

▲ *RHODODENDRON* 'PEKOE'
If grown in deep shade, azaleas will not flower well, but in dappled woodland, as here, the conditions are ideal and the flowers will last longer.

▼ *FATSIA JAPONICA*
Grown chiefly for their handsome, bold leaves, fatsias, like their close relatives the ivies, will grow in deep shade and once established will tolerate quite dry soil.

PLANTS FOR DEEP SHADE

Camellia japonica, *C.* × *williamsii*
Daphne laureola
Elaeagnus × *ebbingei*
Fatsia japonica
Hypericum calycinum
Mahonia aquifolium
Nandina domestica
Osmanthus heterophyllus
Periwinkle (*Vinca minor*)
Rhododendrons
Sarcococca
Skimmias
For details of these plants and others, see *Recommended Flowering Shrubs*, pp.64–65.

SHRUBS FOR WALLS

ALTHOUGH CLIMBERS are more associated with growing on walls, shrubs can give more substance and year-round interest. Garden and house walls are ideal sites for certain shrubs that are either too sensitive to cold for the rest of the garden or whose flexible stems benefit from support. These wall shrubs can also be used as supports for other climbers, such as clematis, to twine through.

SUITABLE SHRUBS

Shrubs can both enhance and camouflage vertical surfaces, whether simply grown alongside garden boundaries and buildings to break up straight lines, or trained, either loosely or more formally, against walls and fences. You must choose shrubs carefully if you intend to tie them in. Many shrubs with a floppy or scrambling habit look neater and gain more height if main stems are loosely tied in against a support, but not all are suitable; and only certain shrubs will tolerate the manipulation and pruning necesary for formal fan- or espalier-training and still grow and flower well. (*See* Recommended Flowering Shrubs, *pp.60–63*, for some suitable choices.) You must also ensure that the wall or fence can support both the weight of the shrub and its supports, such as trellis or wiring.

CALLISTEMON RIGIDUS
Native to Australia, callistemons relish hot and dry conditions. They lend themselves to growing against walls, either as free-standing shrubs or informally but carefully tied in. Even against a warm wall, callistemons are not suitable for very cold regions.

WALL-TRAINED
PYRACANTHA
*Pyracanthas (here
'Watereri') can be
clipped to within
30cm of a wall and
are very suitable for
cold areas. Their
clusters of small white
flowers are followed
by bunches of red,
orange or yellow
berries, according to
the variety.
Pyracanthas can be
clipped tightly enough
to frame windows
and doors attractively,
and should be pruned
in mid-summer and in
late winter.*

CHALLENGING YOUR CLIMATE

If you have a cold garden you may find that a wall or fence provides a surprisingly mild microclimate that will allow you to grow more tender shrubs. A blanket of horticultural fleece or dry mulch of straw at the base can help get such plants through the winter in borderline areas, or if the weather becomes unusually cold. Walls can not only give shelter from cold winds

> Not all walls provide
> shelter: some are cold
> and windy

but also hold and reflect heat, encouraging some shrubs to flower more profusely. However, not all vertical surfaces are "warm"; it depends on aspect, and on how much sun is received and at what time of day, so check this out before choosing a shrub. Check also whether (as often happens with north- and south-facing walls) there are cross-winds that could buffet plants. "Cold" walls, however, need

not be problematic. A warm wall that is in sun from midday onwards may be perfect for some warm-climate plants – abutilons, ceanothus, carpenterias and fremontodendron – but too intensely hot, say, for a camellia. Camellias need some shelter, however; pyracantha, chaenomeles and cotoneasters are good, tough choices for a cold or windy wall.

PLANTING DISTANCES

It is important to decide whether you are simply going to grow the shrub free-standing in the shelter of the wall, or actually tie it in, as this will affect where you plant it. Even shrubs that are going to be trained in (*see p.36*) need to be planted some distance from the wall, especially those that get top-heavy but dislike too much pruning, such as evergreen ceanothus. This will also lessen the effects of "rain shadow" at the wall's base, where the soil can get very dry, particularly where eaves and gutters overhang.

Rain shadow can be used to advantage in wet areas if you want to grow shrubs that like arid spots, such as callistemons, but in other cases, improve the moisture-retentiveness of the soil before planting (*see p.28*), and ensure that shrubs get enough water.

SHRUBS FOR FRAGRANCE

THE MOST PRECIOUS QUALITY a plant can have apart from colour is fragrance. Indeed, there are many shrubs that have fairly insignificant flowers but whose fragrance makes them worthy of inclusion in any garden. Other than its obvious appeal to us, fragrance is designed to attract pollinating insects, so scented flowers will lure visitors both pretty and useful to the garden. Fragrance is also essential in gardens designed and planted for the visually impaired.

SHRUBS WITH SWEET SCENTS

Plant fragrant shrubs near doors, patios and paths, but use them too in out-of-the-way corners to surprise the senses. There is a mysterious, even elusive quality to some scents: the small evergreen *Sarcococca*, or Christmas box, has a fragrance that can carry for extraordinary distances despite its diminutive size.

Use fragrant shrubs, also, to attract wildlife into your garden. The few late winter- and early spring-blooming shrubs like mahonias, hamamelis and viburnums often have powerfully perfumed flowers to attract the few early flying insects that are abroad, but by late spring and summer, shrubs unleash a host of scents into the garden to vie for the pollinators' attentions.

Lure butterflies in
search of nectar with
scented flowers

Use them to create havens of fragrance to enhance summer days and evenings: many scents intensify when the weather is warm and slightly humid, and often persist into dusk. A bank or pot of lavender by a path or seating area, buzzing with bees, is for many people the epitome of summer sensations; the heat bounced back by paving and gravel heightens the aromatic qualities of sun-loving shrubs such as lavender, rosemary and *Cistus ladanifer*, all of which have scented foliage, too.

FRAGRANT FLOWERS FOR WILDLIFE
Buddleja davidii *is well-named the "butterfly bush". Butterflies, especially the peacock, love the purple flowers of the common form, but this white-flowered variety attracts them too.*

◄ *MAHONIA ×*
MEDIA 'UNDERWAY'
The bright, honey-
scented flowers of
mahonias are a treat
when summer is far
away: there are
varieties that flower
at both ends of the
winter season.

▼ *DAPHNE ×*
BURKWOODII
Daphnes are not
the easiest of
shrubs to grow (this
is one of the least
temperamental), but
if you can make
them thrive in your
garden, you will be
rewarded by one of
the most exquisite
flower scents.

TOP SHRUBS FOR SCENT

LATE WINTER AND SPRING

Chimonanthus praecox
Daphnes
Hamamelis mollis
Honeysuckles, such as *Lonicera fragrantissima*
Osmanthus
Prunus mume
Rhododendron luteum
Sarcococca
Viburnum × burkwoodii and other viburnums

SUMMER AND AUTUMN

Abelia × grandiflora
Buddlejas
Elaeagnus angustifolia
Lavenders (*Lavandula*)
Lilac (*Syringa*)
Mexican orange blossom (*Choisya ternata*)
Philadelphus
Pineapple broom (*Cytisus battandieri*)

For details of these shrubs and others, see
Recommended Flowering Shrubs, pp.52–55.

EXPOSED AND WINDY SITES

A N EXPOSED GARDEN, OR PART OF A GARDEN, may offer inhospitable conditions to plants, leaving them open to cold, drying winds and frost or, in coastal regions, to mild but salt-laden gales. Such conditions may not only damage vulnerable plants, but also distort their growth. You can, however, choose shrubs that will stand up well, avoiding those native to sheltered woodland, for example, and selecting those that have adapted themselves to blustery climates.

NATURAL ADAPTATION

Plants that are naturally equipped to withstand drying winds tend, in general, to have small leaves. Grey or silver leaves, often with the stems and foliage covered in fine hairs, also often indicate suitable plants, as does succulent growth, in which water reserves are guarded by thick, tough leaf and stem surfaces.

In cold and moderately windy gardens, tough, hardy garden shrubs such as philadelphus, cotinus, viburnums and even *Hydrangea paniculata* should do well, and also give some shelter to plants below and among them; where the climate is mild and heavy frosts are uncommon, lavenders, hebes and helianthemums can be added to

the list. But in cold sites that are regularly buffeted by strong winds, choose plants that are naturally found growing on mountain- and hillsides where the wind is incessant: small-leaved cotoneasters, berberis, heathers such as *Calluna* and *Erica*, pyracanthas, and brooms such as *Genista hispanica* and *Cytisus scoparius*. There are also many alpine rhododendrons.

COASTAL CLIMATES

Perhaps the most problematic gardens are those close to the sea, exposed to salt-laden winds that can burn leaves and bark, killing shrubs. For these gardens, choose shrubs that are highly specialized, many of them from the Mediterranean: lavender,

▲ *ROSMARINUS OFFICINALIS* 'MISS JESSOPP'S UPRIGHT' *Mediterranean plants tolerate dry soil and warm sea winds.*

▶ *HEBE* 'GREAT ORME' *Small, leathery leaves minimize water loss by evaporation in drying winds.*

TAMARIX RAMOSISSIMA This summer-flowering tamarisk has small, thin, scale-like leaves, making it highly resistant to salt winds. In nature, wind distorts the growth of its wispy stems, leading to an ungainly shape; they respond well to pruning, however, having adapted well to tolerate the loss of branches broken by gales.

santolina, tamarisk and *Phlomis fruticosa*. None of these plants will thrive in very cold areas: for these, *Prunus spinosa*, *Hydrangea macrophylla* and *Amelanchier* are useful. Some of the shrub roses, such as *Rosa rugosa*, are also well adapted to seaside gardens and can be used to supplement other flowering shrubs.

Seaside gardens need shrubs that are naturally resistant to salt winds

Remember that wind, whether mild or cold, is very drying. Water young plants regularly and well. If soil erosion and drying are a problem, use mulches of loose stones. These can also create decorative and naturalistic effects: use rocky scree between moorland heathers, for example, or gravel between seaside shrubs.

SCREENING AND SHELTER

When buying young shrubs for a windy site, choose small, robust, bushy specimens that will stand up well to battering by wind while they establish. Prune back any long, slender stems on planting. If you have to or want to start off with taller plants, it is worth giving them a short stake for support in the early years, but tie them in loosely, so that their stems may build up strength by flexing a little in the wind. You should also erect a temporary screen for them, but choose an open material, such as hessian or plastic strips or mesh between posts, that will break up the wind rather than blocking it, otherwise the shrubs will grow up over-protected.

Shrubs that are especially good for planting in rows as hedging and screening, protecting other plants in exposed gardens, include *Hippophae rhamnoides*, *Berberis thunbergii*, *Prunus spinosa* and *P. cistena*, kerria and *Elaeagnus commutata*, and in mild areas, olearias, escallonias, cotinus, spiraea and *Hamamelis virginiana*. For more details of wind-resistant shrubs, see *Recommended Flowering Shrubs, pp.66–69*.

LOOKING AFTER SHRUBS

WHICH SHRUB WHERE?

Before you buy any flowering shrub, consider where you want to plant it and the conditions that prevail there. Is the position windy or sheltered, in full sun or shade? Is your soil fairly "ordinary" or is it, for example, very dry or acidic (*pp.16–17*)? These factors influence which shrubs you choose because, to put on their best show, they must have growing conditions to suit their needs.

CHOOSING HEALTHY PLANTS

Container-grown shrubs can be bought and planted at almost any time of year, but if you can, choose autumn or spring to plant, when mild weather will not stress the young shrub too much. Shrubs may also be sold with their roots wrapped in polythene with a little compost. These can make perfectly good plants, but check that the roots have not dried out, and plant without delay. Buy ideally when plants first appear on the shelves, not after they have been sitting under hot store lights for some time.

BUYING TIPS

• Look for a shrub with an attractive, well-balanced shape and plenty of new growth. Check that shoot tips are healthy with no sign of scorch or dieback.
• Roots should be well established and healthy but not protrude from the base of the pot.
• The best time to plant shrubs that are fully hardy in your climate is autumn. For more tender shrubs wait until the spring, lessening the risk of winter damage.
• Avoid buying shrubs in flower. Flowers will sap the energy of the plant while it is getting established and should be removed.

Fresh new growth with healthy shoot tips

Stems are evenly spaced and branch close to ground level

Make sure that shrub has been labelled properly

A GOOD PLANT
This specimen has plentiful, healthy foliage and lots of new growth. The stems are well-placed and the pot is a good size for the amount of top growth; avoid top-heavy plants.

◄ WELL SHAPED *An attractive form enhances the flowers of* Viburnum plicatum *'Mariesii'.*

PLANTING AND AFTERCARE

ONCE YOU HAVE CHOSEN A SHRUB and the place to plant it, prepare the soil well. This is where the plant is likely to be all its life; good preparation gives it a good start and makes it more able to grow strongly. Container-grown shrubs have a pampered existence and when planted, their roots find it hard to penetrate lumpy, uneven, and especially heavy soil; they can stop growing. Do what you can to make their new home conducive to growth.

PLANTING A SHRUB

Improve soil texture around the new shrub's rootball to make it crumbly and moisture-retentive, but well-firmed and without air pockets. Make a large hole, and chop up lumps in the soil at the base and around the side; do the same with the soil you refill the hole with. Mix in one or two shovels of organic matter: well-rotted compost or old, spent potting or mushroom compost. Well-rotted manure is excellent, but not in clods, which often dry out and harden underground. A handful of bonemeal or pelleted chicken manure adds long-lasting nutrients to the soil.

1 **Dig the hole** twice as wide and deep as the plant's pot, and break up the soil at the base and around the sides, working in organic matter. Water the plant in its pot.

2 **To ensure that** the root ball doesn't collapse, place your hand flat across the top of the root ball and ease off the pot, then cup your other hand under the root ball.

3 **Adjust the depth** of the hole until the plant sits correctly. Use a cane to make sure that you plant the shrub at the same depth as it was in its container.

4 **Break up the soil** that you dug out of the hole, then shovel it in around the roots. Firm well and evenly all around the plant before watering thoroughly and mulching.

PLANTING A SHRUB IN A CONTAINER

Planting shrubs in containers means that you can tailor the compost to meet needs that your soil cannot: for example, azaleas can be given ericaceous compost, and thus be grown even in a chalky area. The same lime-free compost enables blue-flowered hydrangeas to keep their colour. For the long term and for the pot's stability, it is better to use a heavier loam-based compost, with a slow-release fertilizer. Don't put a small shrub into a large container, hoping that it will eventually fill it; plants grow more strongly in pots only one or two sizes up from their previous home, large enough to sustain the shrub through at least one year, when it can be potted on. Vigorous shrubs need annual feeding, and all container plants require regular watering and good drainage.

Growth usually pauses while the shrub re-establishes

New pot one size up from the old one

ROOM TO GROW
Gradually give young shrubs larger pots in which their roots can expand. Crocks in the bottom of the pot and "pot feet" prevent waterlogging.

WATERING AND MULCHING

All shrubs, even those that are drought-tolerant, need watering during dry spells in their first two or three years. It is better to water plentifully once or twice a week than give frequent small doses. A 5–10cm layer of mulch on damp soil round the shrub retains moisture and keeps roots cool: use leafmould, bark chips or well-rotted manure.

MAKING A WATERING BASIN
After planting, make a ridge of soil around the area of the shrub's rootball to hold water while it sinks down to the roots. Do not do this on heavy soils prone to waterlogging.

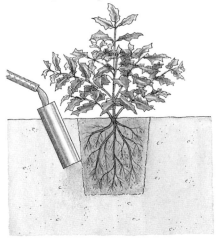

ADDING A WATERING PIPE
Burying a length of drainpipe near the plant and filling it with water from a hose will ensure the water reaches the bottom of the rootball. Water the soil surface as well.

ROUTINE PRUNING

THERE IS LITTLE NEED, usually, to prune healthy young shrubs. However, after one or two growing seasons, there may be unwanted stems to remove. You may need to make only those cuts that keep the plant healthy and well-formed (as on these pages) or choose to prune additionally each year to enhance flowering (see overleaf). Not all shrubs need or enjoy the latter type of pruning: many will flower for years unpruned and naturally groom themselves.

MAKING CORRECT CUTS

Whenever you prune a shrub, whether to remove damage or spent flowers, or simply to cut a stem to bring into the house for its flowers or foliage, get into the habit of making well-positioned, clean cuts. If you leave snags they may die back (*see below*), attracting disease. New shoots will grow from the buds you cut to, so look at which way alternate buds face to make the stem grow upwards or outwards.

OPPOSITE BUDS
Cut straight through the stem just above a pair of buds, leaves or sideshoots.

ALTERNATE BUDS
Prune just above a bud, leaf or shoot with a slightly sloping cut, angled toward it.

CUTTING OUT BRANCHES
Don't strain secateurs on thick stems: a pair of loppers makes the task much easier.

PRUNING FOR HEALTH

Cut back any stems you see that are dead, damaged or looking very unhealthy, and you may be able to stop problems spreading. Cut them across cleanly at a suitable point well below the affected part: at the base, or where they spring from a larger branch, or to just above a healthy sideshoot, leaf or bud.

Tender shoot tip killed by frost

Pruning cut was made too high above buds

▶ FROST DAMAGE
This frost-scorched shoot tip will not recover. Prune it back to just above some completely healthy leaves.

▲ DEAD STUB
Dieback often halts naturally at new shoots: trim off any dead snags.

Pruning to Shape

Most shrubs, left to their own devices, will develop a natural form that requires little or no attention. In the garden, however, shrubs may outgrow their position or become one-sided from being crowded by other shrubs or shaded by buildings. Some, especially evergreens, may develop leggy branches that spoil their neat shape. Don't be overzealous about pruning out stems unless they really get in the way, offend the eye, or look as if wind and weather might break them. Also, never trim a flowering shrub all over in an effort to reduce its size, as you may well be removing the next season's flowers. If it's too big, consider a naturally smaller replacement.

◄ OVERLONG SHOOT   ▲ SPRAWLING STEMS
Prune back protruding branches deep within the shrub, leaving the fresh cut hidden.   *Pruning low down may encourage fresh growth to replace bare, leggy branches.*

Thinning an Overgrown Shrub

The branches of many shrubs, including philadelphus, weigela, forsythia, *Viburnum opulus* and lilac, can become too crowded: many of the lower and inner branches become old and woody, and the flowers appear too high up on the shrub. Thinning lets in more air and light, encouraging fresh shoots to flower lower down on the shrub. A really old, neglected shrub is probably best replaced, unless it is one of the few that tolerate drastic pruning (*below*); this will mean the loss of that year's flowers.

THINNING THICKETS
Prune out thick, old branches from the centre of the shrub to encourage young stems.

LIGHTENING DENSE GROWTH
Cut back longer, thicker main stems at the junction with healthy-looking sideshoots.

DRASTIC PRUNING

Shrubs that can be cut right down in late winter:

Chaenomeles
Clethra
Cotoneasters
Deutzias
Escallonias
Forsythias
Hydrangea paniculata
Lavateras
Lilac (*Syringa*)
Philadelphus
Ribes sanguineum
Spiraea
Viburnum opulus

PRUNING FOR FLOWERING

PRUNING CAN ENCOURAGE shrubs to either flower more profusely or to carry larger blooms, but not all shrubs need or tolerate this (*right*) and should only be pruned when necessary (*see previous pages*). Most pruning for better flowers is carried out after flowering. For spring-flowering shrubs, this is best done in early summer but for late-flowerers, delay pruning in cold climates until late winter.

NO PRUNING NECESSARY

The following do not need pruning apart from essential cuts made for their health: **Hibiscus syriacus; Hydrangea villosa, H. aspera; Kolkwitsia amabilis; Viburnum carlesii, V. burkwoodii, V. juddii;** camellias (deadhead only to tidy); **Choisya ternata;** magnolias; osmanthus; mahonias (tall stems can be pruned hard occasionally to reshape); most **prunus; skimmias; cistus** (often resent pruning); **hamamelis; daphnes** (should never be pruned unless absolutely necessary).

DEADHEADING TO PROLONG FLOWERING

Deadheading is the removal of spent flower heads before they set seed; this takes energy from the plant and also persuades it that there is no need to flower further. Deadheading redirects the plant's energies into new growth. This new growth will support the next flush of blooms, either later in the same season or the next year. The prevention of nuisance self-seeding of, for example, buddlejas, is a bonus.

PINCHING OUT
Rhododendron and camellia flowers open in succession on very short, almost non-existent stalks. Pinch and twist out the dead flowers very carefully between finger and thumb to avoid damaging other flower and leaf buds behind them.

Make clean cuts with secateurs

CUTTING BACK FLOWERED STEMS
Buddlejas flower well into late summer, albeit in smaller clusters, if you cut off spent blooms just above the next pair of sideshoots.

SHRUBS THAT FLOWER BETTER IF DEADHEADED

When deadheading the following shrubs, always use secateurs and prune cleanly back to healthy sideshoots, leaves or buds (*see p.30*).
Buddleja davidii
Caryopteris
Ceanothus, only the late-flowering deciduous types like 'Gloire de Versailles' and 'Marie Simon'
Choisyas often have a second flowering if you cut back flowered stems by 15cm
Clethra alnifolia
Hydrangea macrophylla,
H. paniculata
Lavenders (trim over the whole plant with shears)
Lespedeza thunbergii
Lilacs (*Syringa*)
Spiraeas, only the late-flowering types such as *S. japonica*

PRUNING SHRUBS THAT FLOWER ON OLD WOOD

Shrubs that flower in the spring or early summer develop their embryonic flower buds on stems that have grown and ripened in the previous summer's warmth, so if you cut back these stems in winter or early spring, you will be removing potential flowering stems. All green-leaved evergreens flower in this way, but so do many deciduous shrubs; forsythia is a classic example (*see right and below*). Prune these shrubs immediately after flowering, in the spring or early summer. Pruning should not be done later than early summer; otherwise, the new growth that pruning encourages will not have enough time to grow and ripen, to bloom the next year.

Spent flowers on previous year's shoots

New shoots

LAST YEAR'S LEGACY
Forsythia is a typical example of a plant that flowers on old wood, well before the new season's shoots start to grow.

PRUNE AFTER FLOWERING

Deciduous shrubs that flower on last year's wood and can be pruned as below include:
Forsythias, can be hard pruned or trimmed, or a mixture of both, as below.
Philadelphus
Syringa Prune if overgrown, or just deadhead.
Spiraea, the spring-flowering types.
Deutzias
Kolkwitzia
Chaenomeles, grown as freestanding shrubs.
Pieris

Immediately after flowering the new growth will have already started. Prune long, old flowered shoots back to a vigorous-looking sideshoot.

Once the shrub is 3 or 4 years old, take one to three of the oldest main stems out each year, pruning right to the base of the shrub.

Cut out all weak and spindly growth that crosses other branches. This growth can often die inside the shrub for lack of light.

PRUNING SHRUBS THAT FLOWER ON NEW WOOD

On many shrubs, new shoots grow from the old wood and flower all in one season. You can prune after flowering but, in colder climates, it is best to wait until the worst of winter is over. With some, you may prune lightly or, for fewer but larger flowers, prune hard. Others, especially some small grey-leaved shrubs (*see facing page*), should be treated almost like herbaceous perennials and pruned close to the ground.

FLOWERING ON NEW WOOD

Buddleja davidii Prune down to a main stump 60cm-1m tall (*see facing page*).
Ceanothus, deciduous kinds Can be hard-pruned to encourage fewer but more vigorous flowering stems.
Mophead hydrangeas (*H. macrophylla*) Prune back to about half the previous height (*below*), varying heights of different stems:
Hydrangea paniculata Can be hard pruned like buddleja, or down to new, healthy buds as they break, like the mopheads.
Hypericums can be hard or lightly pruned

Prune the following back to 15cm from the ground:
Fuchsias, the fully hardy types such as
F. magellanica
Indigofera heterantha
Lespedeza thunbergii
Perovskia atriplicifolia
Spiraeas, the late summer-flowering types

NEW GROWTH
Shrubs that flower on new growth can usually be identified by the fact that they bloom from midsummer onwards, at the tips of fresh young shoots – like this Buddleja × weyeriana.

PRUNING *HYDRANGEA MACROPHYLLA*
The stems of mophead hydrangeas should be cut back to the first really healthy pair of fat, rounded buds, which show in late winter or early spring. Remove any weak, unhealthy shoots completely.

Using sharp secateurs, prune to just above a pair of large, rounded buds, removing the old dried flowerheads.

Prune out all thin, spindly wood and dead twigs.

Remove close to the ground all woody stems that are over 3 or 4 years old

PRUNING *BUDDLEJA DAVIDII*
Butterfly bushes are very vigorous, and can produce new shoots 2m tall and more in a single season, even when pruned to within 60cm of the ground. You don't have to prune them, but it does give you a more manageable shrub with big, fat flower spikes.

Prune back all stems that grew the previous year, to healthy breaking buds if you can see them.

Cut out very old woody stumps from previous years with loppers or a saw.

SMALL GREY-LEAVED SHRUBS

Many smaller grey-leaved shrubs have been bred from coastal plants that are cut back naturally by salt winds, so they usually flower, for safety, on new stems. However, not all respond well to being cut hard back into bare wood, like a *Buddleja davidii*. Regular trimming will keep them in good shape, but if they get very old and leggy, they are usually best replaced.

PRUNE LIGHTLY
Trim lavender over lightly after flowering and again in early spring, but leave plenty of leafy growth: hard pruning is risky.

PRUNE HARD
Santolina can be pruned hard to within 15cm of the ground in spring, and trimmed throughout the summer.

Plants that should be trimmed:
Calluna • Cytisus • Erica • Genista • *Helichrysum splendidum* • Lavender • Leptospermum • Olearia • Potentilla • Rosemary

Plants that can be cut back hard:
Brachyglottis 'Sunshine' • Caryopteris • Ceratostigma • *Elaeagnus angustifolia* • *Phlomis fruticosa* • Perovskia • Santolina (not *S. chamaecyparissus*)

WALL-TRAINING SHRUBS

TRAINING A SHRUB closely against a wall or fence, so that it grows flat, involves some regular pruning and only some shrubs will tolerate this and still flower well. Fan- or espalier-training is particularly useful where there is only a narrow area of ground. Remember that the soil by a wall may be poor and dry, and builder's rubble may be present, so work in organic matter (*see p.28*) before planting.

FOR WALL-TRAINING

Abutilon megapotamicum
Chaenomeles speciosa
Ceanothus, most upright evergreen types
Cotoneasters, the small-leaved kinds
Forsythia suspensa, a pendulous shrub
Garrya elliptica
Itea ilicifolia
Magnolia grandiflora
Pyracantha, most
See Recommended Flowering Shrubs *pp.60–63.*

TRAINING IN A NEW YOUNG SHRUB

Have supports such as trellis or wires, strong enough to support the mature shrub, in place before planting. Choose a plant that seems naturally to grow in one plane; choose its "best" side to face outwards, and cut off any shoots that stick out behind. Plant the shrub (*see p.28*) 30–45cm from the wall. Splay all sideways-growing branches out evenly, gently pulling them down as far towards the horizontal as they will safely go, and tie in. Do not push or tuck shoots behind struts or wires; they may be damaged and, as they thicken, they will push the support away from the wall and be difficult to prune out. Prune away any superfluous or forward-facing shoots.

Tie in the stems (here of a ceanothus), not too tight, with garden twine in figure-of-eight knots.

Prune the tips of the tied-in stems to encourage denser growth.

Remove any shoots that stick out in front.

Cut off shoots at the base of the shrub.

PRUNING AN ESTABLISHED WALL-TRAINED SHRUB

Taking care to prune at the right time of year for each shrub, encourage the shrub to stay flat to the wall and not too sparse in the middle. Remove any growth that crosses over other shoots and cut the tips off lateral and vertical shoots. Some shrubs, like chaenomeles, are easy to train and can be pruned quite hard once a year. Too much pruning can damage plants like ceanothus and hinder their flowering, and in others induce too much leafy growth. Pruning lightly in late winter and summer will tame this sort of growth.

Spur-pruned stem

Unpruned stem

SPUR-PRUNING
Some shrubs that flower on old wood, like chaenomeles and pyracanthas, respond well if, in summer, you shorten their leafy new shoots; they flower better, and flowers and fruits are shown off well. This makes them ideal for wall-training.

Prune sideshoots back to two or three leaves or buds, depending on the time of year.

Cut out forward-facing shoots that cannot be trained sideways and tied in without crowding.

Tie in stems as they grow

Trim shoots where they grow beyond the shrub's allotted space.

RECOMMENDED FLOWERING SHRUBS

CHOOSING PLANTS

THE RANGE OF SHRUBS here has been divided into various categories, but there is plenty of overlap. For example, many of the *Evergreen Favourites* will tolerate some shade, while *Shrubs for Shade* includes only those plants that actually prefer less light. Average heights for the most popular types of each shrub have been given, but check labels before you buy to ensure that you have not picked a dwarf or especially vigorous kind.

THE CATEGORIES

- **Deciduous** and **Evergreen Favourites** contain easy-going garden classics.
- **Fragrant Shrubs** includes the best for scent.
- **Shrubs for Shade** and for **Acid Soil** contain problem-solving shrubs for special conditions.
- **Shrubs for Walls** may be formally fan- or espalier-trained or loosely tied in; some need a sheltered position.
- **Shrubs for Windy Gardens** that need mild coastal conditions are also good for **Dry Sites**; others will stand up to cold winds.
- **Shrubs for Containers** contains small or particularly suitable types of the shrubs mentioned in previous categories, nearly all with the *RHS Award of Garden Merit* ♔.

SUITING THE SITE
Use this selection of recommended shrubs to match plants to your garden conditions and the site you have in mind, or to see whether a favourite plant can be given a suitable home somewhere in your plot. Shrubs are great low-maintenance plants for the backs of borders, near walls and fences, where other plants might be difficult to tend, and this ceanothus, 'Puget Blue' ♔, also benefits from the shelter of the garden wall.

◀PLANNING THE YEAR *Shrubs such as caryopteris 'Arthur Simmonds' flower into late summer.*

DECIDUOUS FAVOURITES

BUDDLEJA

Most buddlejas grow about 3m tall, with an arching habit, although there is a dwarf, **B. davidii** var. **nanhoensis**. They like full sun and well-drained soil but are otherwise unfussy. **B. davidii** is the most popular, with big spikes of fragrant blooms on the new season's stems (*see* '**Fascinating**', *p.6*). Prune them hard in early spring (*see p.35*). Flowers are mauve, white, pink, blue or reddish-purple; '**White Profusion**' ♀ (*see p.22*), '**Pink Delight**' ♀, '**Empire Blue**' ♀ and '**Royal Red**' ♀ are recommended.

Another option is **Buddleja alternifolia** ♀ (*below*), spring-flowering, with small greyish leaves and bunches of tiny lilac-purple flowers all along long arching stems that grew the previous year, so this buddleja must be pruned as for shrubs that flower on old, not new wood (*see p.33*).

BUDDLEJA ALTERNIFOLIA ♀

CHAENOMELES

Easily grown on all except wet soils as free-standing shrubs, about 2.5m tall, chaenomeles (also called flowering quince or japonica) are also often wall-trained; **C. speciosa** types are best for this (*see p.60*). Clustered, apple-blossom-like flowers on short, stubby twigs all along the branches open in late winter and early spring, in red, pinks or, in '**Nivalis**', snow-white. For a small form, look for '**Geisha Girl**', with sugar-pink flowers. **C. × superba** '**Crimson and Gold**' ♀ (*below*) is one of the most striking, with cupped flowers of a very bright scarlet and a more bushy, thicket-like habit. Chaenomeles flower on old wood, and can be pruned, hard if necessary, to shape or to thin after flowering (*see p.31*). In summer, shortening new leafy shoots (*see p.37*) encourages more flowers.

CHAENOMELES × SUPERBA
'CRIMSON AND GOLD' ♀

DEUTZIA

Deutzias are hardy, easy-to-grow shrubs, typically around 1.5m tall, for sun or partial shade and any fertile soil. In shade they still flower well, and develop an attractive, open habit. Prune some old stems to the base of the shrub after flowering (*see p.33*). **D. × elegantissima** '**Rosealind**' ♀ (*below*) is compact, with erect sprays of rose-pink flowers in early summer. There are many other deutzias, flowering in either pink or white. Choose **D. gracilis** for white flowers. Other good pink-flowered deutzias are '**Mont Rose**' ♀, with warm-toned flowers freely borne on a graceful bush, and **D. × rosea** '**Carminea**' ♀, with pale rose-pink flowers. Both have purplish buds. **D. × magnifica** is a taller shrub, with double pink flowers set densely along the branches.

DEUTZIA × ELEGANTISSIMA
'ROSEALIND' ♀

FORSYTHIA

Forsythias are rather awkwardly shaped shrubs of varying sizes, but much valued for their cheery yellow, frost-resistant flowers all along the bare twigs in late winter and early spring. If pruned regularly after flowering (*see p.33*), the flowers, on sideshoots from old wood, can smother the entire bush. They may also be left unpruned. Forsythias thrive in most soils in sun or shade. In shade they develop a more open, elegant habit with sparser flowering, which some find more attractive. There are many hybrid forsythias bred for bigger, brighter flowers, such as the *F.* × *intermedia* types: 'Lynwood' ♥, with a very dense habit, 'Arnold Giant' ♥ (*see p.7*) and 'Arnold Dwarf'. *F. suspensa* ♥ (*below*) has much paler yellow flowers, and a rather lax, pendulous habit. Over 2m high and wide, it can be tied against a wall to stop it sprawling.

FUCHSIA

The hardy fuchsias are beautiful garden plants, but do need protection in cold gardens with a blanket of dry straw, compost or even a mound of soil over winter. They also make good container shrubs (*see p.75*), which can be moved under cover. In mild areas, *F. magellanica* (*below*) may retain its woody framework over winter, but it is more usually cut down by frost; not a problem, since the shrub can be pruned low and will reshoot from ground level, growing to 1.5m tall. It mixes well with herbaceous plantings, doing best in full sun though tolerating light or part-day shade. Among the best are the varieties *versicolor* ♥, with white and silvery pink leaf markings that contrast beautifully with the red and purple of the flowers, and *molinae*, with pink flowers; 'Genii' ♥, with golden leaves; and white-flowered 'Hawkshead'.

HIBISCUS

Erect shrubs, growing quite slowly up to 3m tall, bearing large, trumpet-shaped flowers in mid- to late summer and occasionally into autumn. The leaves are deeply lobed and dark green. *H. syriacus* is hardy, but it must have abundant sunshine to flower best, so should be planted in full sun. *H. rosa-sinensis* needs a warmer climate. Both make good container plants (*see p.75*).

H. syriacus types respond well to pruning to shape in early spring before the buds break. They thrive best in most well-drained soils. 'Diana' ♥ (*below*) is one of the largest-flowered hybrids. 'Jeanne d'Arc' is a semi-double white. 'Blue Bird' ♥ (*see p.6*), also called 'Oiseau Bleu', is a clear lavender-blue, while 'Woodbridge' ♥ has darker crimson flowers. Many of them, like 'Blue Bird' and the white 'Red Heart' ♥, have maroon veins and blotches at the petal bases.

FORSYTHIA SUSPENSA ♥

FUCHSIA MAGELLANICA

HIBISCUS SYRIACUS 'DIANA' ♥

HYDRANGEA

Hydrangeas are versatile shrubs, growing in almost any soil or position. Some in particular are excellent for shade (*see p.64*). The most popular all-rounders for borders or containers (*see p.76*) are the macrophyllas: rounded, up to 2m tall, with lacecap or mophead flowers, in white (try **'Lanarth White'** ♥ or **'Madame Emile Mouillère'** ♥, with a pink eye), pink (**'King George'** is good) or, on acid soil only, blue (look for **'Blue Wave'** ♥ and **'Nikko Blue'**). Prune them in late winter (*see p.34*). *H. paniculata* is another fine shrub for all-round garden use; very hardy, up to 3m tall, or prune it hard in late winter to keep at only 2m. Flowering on new wood, it produces dense cones of white florets, especially large and striking in **'Grandiflora'** ♥, and in **'Pink Diamond'** (*below*) quickly turning pink as they fade. The dried, brown flowerheads look decorative in winter.

HYDRANGEA PANICULATA 'PINK DIAMOND'

INDIGOFERA

Although not startling plants, indigoferas are elegant, useful in dry gardens, and flower when few other shrubs do. In winter, they can be cut down by cold but spring up again from the base, flowering on the current season's growth. Thus they can pruned hard in late winter or, in warmer regions, left unpruned to form taller, open shrubs. *I. heterantha* ♥ grows up to 3m tall. It may carry its mauve-pink flowers well into late summer. *I. decora* (*below*) is slender and open-growing, for a sunny site and any well-drained soil, doing especially well on dry ground. It has arching shoots up to 2m tall, with pretty, lush leaflets and sprays of small, pinky-purple pea-like flowers in mid-summer. Indigoferas blend well with grasses or hardy fuchsias. The flowers look lovely set against dark purple foliage; try growing with *Cotinus coggygria* 'Royal Purple' ♥.

INDIGOFERA DECORA

KERRIA

An old cottage garden favourite, *Kerria japonica* is a charming, twiggy dense bush, about 2m tall, with buttercup-yellow flowers in spring. The stems are upright, wiry and bright green, and the leaves are fresh and pointed. Although deciduous, its bright stems look good in winter. Very hardy and tolerant of most soil types, including very alkaline soil, it flowers well in some shade. There are kerrias with silver- and golden-variegated leaves. The former, 'Picta', is a small bush, a little more vulnerable to cold in winter. **'Golden Guinea'** ♥ (*below*) has very large flowers. The double-flowered kerria, **'Pleniflora'** ♥, actually arrived in the West from China before the species. It is a much more vigorous shrub with a habit of "suckering" all around the main plant: this can become a nuisance. The double flowers do, however, last longer.

KERRIA JAPONICA 'GOLDEN GUINEA' ♥

KOLKWITZIA

Sometimes known as the beauty bush, *Kolkwitzia amabilis* is a rounded shrub, growing up to 2.5m tall and wide, with dense twiggy growth that bears clusters of small, pale purplish-pink flowers with yellow throats in late spring. **'Pink Cloud'** ♀ (*below*) has more delicate colouring and is more reliable in its flowering. This and **'Rosea'** are the ones to be sought.

Kolkwitzias are very hardy and grow in any soil, including very alkaline soil. They may take a few years to settle down and really flower well. Spring-flowering shrubs, they should be pruned, once mature, to remove some old wood immediately after flowering each year. Similar in some ways to deutzias and weigelas, kolkwitzias are often grown with these or with shrub roses and lilacs, which all enjoy similar growing conditions, making a fine spring display.

POTENTILLA

Potentilla fruticosa is a small but invaluable, dense, rounded shrub, about 1m tall, carrying small, rose-like flowers through summer. It will grow in any soil, is very hardy, and although happiest in full sun will thrive in partial shade. It can tend to look a little untidy in winter so is best given a trim then, or in early spring. Use shears, removing all the old seedpods and generally neatening it up: this will make it more bushy and improve flowering.

The species has pale yellow flowers, but there are other yellows, pinks, reddish-oranges and white available, most between 60cm and 1.2m tall. Recommended are **'Elizabeth'** ♀, canary yellow, **'Daydawn'** ♀, a light peach, and **'Primrose Beauty'** ♀ (*see p.77*). The hybrid **'Abbotswood'** ♀ has grey-green leaves and pure white flowers. **'Tangerine'** ♀ (*below*) is a soft orange.

PRUNUS

There are several lovely evergreen shrubby *Prunus*  (*see p.50*), but the deciduous types more closely resemble plum and cherry trees. ***Prunus × cistena*** ♀ (*below*) grows up to 1.5m tall, with dark purple foliage that contrasts with the small, pinky-white flowers that open with the leaves in early spring. It grows almost anywhere, but prefers full sun in an open position. It will withstand salt winds, as does the similar beach plum, *P. maritima*. It can be pruned hard, removing old wood, after flowering. *P. mume* flowers even earlier, with fragrant pink-purple flowers all over bare stems, from the new wood down to wood that is 3 or even 4 years old. *P. tenella* **'Fire Hill'** ♀ is more thicket-like in shape, carrying wands of rich pink flowers. *P. triloba* **'Multiplex'** ♀ is a double-flowered, clear pink dwarf cherry, often available grafted onto a short trunk.

KOLKWITZIA AMABILIS 'PINK CLOUD' ♀

POTENTILLA FRUTICOSA 'TANGERINE' ♀

PRUNUS × CISTENA ♀

RIBES

The flowering currants are upright shrubs, mostly about 2m tall, although **R. alpinum**, with greenish-yellow flowers, is much smaller, to 90cm. **R. sanguineum** is a popular early spring-flowering shrub, despite its "catty" scent, with deep rose-pink flowers in small clusters that dangle at first, and later stand up off the upright growth. Hardy, it is a very easy shrub to grow in almost all well-drained soils in sun or partial shade. There are pretty white- and pale pink-flowered varieties; for deep, rich colour try **'King Edward VII'**, lower-growing with crimson flowers, and **'Pulborough Scarlet'** ♀, deep red. **'Brocklebankii'** ♀ (*below*) is golden-leaved; its foliage tends to burn in full sun. Much more sweetly scented is **R. odoratum**, an erect shrub with tiny yellow flowers. **R. speciosum** ♀ has rich red, fuchsia-like flowers in clusters in the early spring; it needs a sheltered spot in cold areas.

RUBUS

The flowers of *Rubus* grown ornamentally are very similar to those of their relatives, the brambles, but in some cases the stems are thornless. Although their stems are long and flexible, they make largely self-supporting plants rather than scrambling through others. **R. 'Benenden'** ♀ (*below*) is a large shrub, up to 3m high and 4m wide, that carries pure white flowers with a central boss of golden-yellow stamens in mid- to late spring. The flowers are produced singly on strong, arching stems, with leaves that are three- to five-lobed. Grow it in any fertile soil, in full sun or partial shade. Spring-flowering, it should be pruned immediately after flowering. For a similar shrub with pink flowers, look for **'Walberton Red'**. **R. thibetanus** ♀ is more erect, with white flowers, beautiful grey leaves and prickly stems with a white bloom.

SPIRAEA

Spiraea japonica is a very robust shrub, hardy, summer-flowering, suiting most soil types and enjoying sun or partial shade. It grows to up to 1.75m tall; many of its cultivars only grow to 1m at most, but have the bonus of beautiful, bright foliage. The pink flowers (white in **var. albiflora**) form in clusters, set against leaves that in **'Goldflame'** ♀ (*below*) are rich yellow-orange fading to orange-green, or in **'Anthony Waterer'** ♀ are bronze when young, then green edged in cream. These spiraeas can be pruned hard in winter to encourage intense leaf colour and keep them compact, and the flowers will still form. Others are spring-flowering, so prune out old wood after flowering. Usually white-flowered, they include **S. 'Arguta'**, small with slender arching branches smothered in tiny white flowers, and **S. × vanhouttei** ♀, similar but a larger, sturdier plant.

RIBES SANGUINEUM 'BROCKLEBANKII' ♀

RUBUS 'BENENDEN' ♀

SPIRAEA JAPONICA 'GOLDFLAME' ♀

VIBURNUM

Most viburnums are fragrant, some intensely so (*see p.55*). Many of the deciduous types have good autumn leaf colour; some, such as *V. opulus*, have bright fruits. They grow in most soils. Height and habit varies, but the flowers are similar in all: small florets in rounded clusters in spring, pure white or flushed pink. After flowering, old wood can be pruned back if necessary.
V. macrocephalum is rounded, to 3m tall. In warm areas it may be semi-evergreen; in cold areas it needs shelter and sun. *V. × carlcephalum* ♀ is similar, but hardier and more shade-tolerant. For a lovely, tiered shape, grow *V. plicatum*, especially 'Lanarth', 'Mariesii' ♀ (*see p.27*), 'Pink Beauty' ♀ (*below*), and 'Summer Snowflake', which flowers later than the others, all to 3m tall, developing graceful, horizontal branches clothed in white or pinkish-white flowers.

VIBURNUM PLICATUM 'PINK BEAUTY' ♀

WEIGELA

Weigelas are very hardy and easy, decorative shrubs growing up to 2m tall and wide, for most soils in either sun or partial shade. They flower in early summer on the previous year's growth, so they should be pruned after flowering (*see p.33*), removing a few old stems to encourage new growth from the base of the shrub. Once mature, they are best pruned every year. For good flower colour, look for 'Eva Rathke' (*below*), slow-growing and and compact; 'Abel Carrière' ♀, with dark pink flowers that gradually fade; and 'Bristol Ruby' with rich crimson flowers. The best white is 'Mont Blanc' ♀. Other weigelas have distinctive foliage, the most popular and harmonious being 'Florida Variegata' ♀, with pink flowers and cream-edged leaves. Low-growing *W. florida* 'Foliis Purpureis' has purple leaves.

WEIGELA 'EVA RATHKE'

MORE CHOICES

Berberis (*see p.66*)
Cotoneaster (*see p.60*)
Genista (*see p.67*)
Lavatera (*see p.71*)
Philadelphus (*see p.54*)
Syringa (*see p.55*)

Ceanothus
Deciduous ceanothus grow well in any well-drained soil, given full sun. They bear flowers in late summer that are similar to those of the evergreens (*see p.60*), but their leaves are larger and often colour well in autumn, and their habit is much more upright and open-branched. They are excellent for mixing in the flower border. They grow up to 3m tall, or can be hard-pruned in early spring for a smaller bush with fewer, showier flowers. Look for 'Gloire de Versailles' ♀ (blue-flowered) and 'Marie Simon' (pink).

Cotinus
Smoke bushes grow to about 3m tall, although the purple-leaved types (*see p.14*) are often pruned hard in spring for a smaller bush with bigger and brighter leaves. Fully hardy and growing well in sun or light shade, in summer they are covered by a haze of tiny pink flowers in summer. The foliage of the green-leaved types colours beautifully in autumn.

Nandina domestica ♀
Sacred bamboo is a clump-forming shrub up to 2m tall for sun or shade, thriving especially in areas with acid soil conditions and hot summers. It bears sprays of white flowers in spring, followed by bright berries, and has airy, divided leaves that are orange-red when young and in autumn.

EVERGREEN FAVOURITES

BERBERIS

Evergreen berberis are valuable, thorny shrubs. *B. darwinii* ♀ (*below*) is perhaps the most beautiful, growing up to 2m tall, with small, shiny, three-pointed leaves, and brilliant orange flowers in spring. In autumn, these are followed by blue-black berries. Berberis are easy to grow, thriving in full sun or shade in any well-drained soil. Some can get leggy, so it is important to prune them after flowering to encourage a more rounded, dense habit. *B.* × *stenophylla* ♀ (*see p.8*) makes an intruder-proof hedge; it has many forms, mostly with orange-yellow flowers. Among the best are 'Irwinii', with a more compact habit, and 'Etna', graceful and free-flowering. For a confined space or tub, *B. buxifolia* 'Pygmaea' is small, no more than 1m tall and wide, with yellow flowers.

CALLISTEMON

Callistemons, all native to Australia, are very distinctive shrubs known as bottlebrushes, with narrow, pointed, evergreen leaves and cylindrical fluffy spikes of flowers throughout summer. Most, such as the popular *C. rigidus* (*see p.20*), have red flowers. *C. pallidus* and *C. salignus* ♀ have creamy yellow flowers. *C. citrinus* 'Splendens' ♀ (*below*) has leaves that are lemon-scented when crushed. The hard, grey, nut-like seedheads remain around the lower stems for years, new flowers being produced above them. Happy in most soils except shallow chalk, callistemons prefer full sun and are remarkably drought-resistant. They can be pruned in early spring. Callistemons are most often seen as free-standing shrubs but, because of their flexible stems, lend themselves to fan-training, tied in to trellis.

CAMELLIA

Camellias are lovely shrubs, most up to 5m tall, with glossy leaves and cup-shaped flowers in many colours in spring. The opening flower buds are prone to frost damage, but there is often a succession of buds to follow. They prefer acid to neutral soil, especially with plenty of organic matter such as leafmould, in open woodland. If grown in full sun, keep the roots moist and cool with an organic mulch. If your soil is limy, grow camellias in pots or tubs (*see p.75*), where they look very handsome, not just in flower, but because their foliage and form is so fine. They make elegant conservatory plants. There are hundreds of varieties of *C. japonica*, mostly flowering in pink, white or red. *C.* × *williamsii* hybrids have a longer flowering season and are ideal for shade (*see p.64*).

BERBERIS DARWINII ♀

CALLISTEMON CITRINUS 'SPLENDENS'

CAMELLIA JAPONICA 'ADOLPHE AUDUSSON' ♀

CHOISYA

Known as
Mexican orange
blossom,
choisyas are
rounded shrubs
with shiny three-lobed leaves,
aromatic when crushed. The
small white flowers, carried in
bunches through late spring
into early summer, are sweetly
fragrant. 'Aztec Pearl' ♀
(below) has narrower leaves
on a slightly smaller plant
than *Choisya ternata* ♀,
which is a luxuriant evergreen
growing up to 2m tall, very
suitable for town gardens
where it enjoys the extra
warmth and shelter. In more
open and colder areas it is
prone to frost damage. It will
grow on most soils and, once
established, is fairly tolerant
of dry conditions. There is no
need to prune unless it gets
too large or ungainly,
especially in shade. Pruning
stems back to new sideshoots
encourages a neater habit.
'Sundance' ♀ has golden new
growth; it is more compact
and slower growing, excellent
for containers (see p.75).

COTONEASTER

Cotoneaster
conspicuus
(below) is
perhaps the
most beautiful
of the small-leaved, evergreen
cotoneasters: a wide-spreading
shrub to 1.5m tall, with
arching growth covered in
tiny white flowers in early
summer; these are much more
conspicuous than on others,
such as *C. horizontalis* ♀ (see
Shrubs for Wall-training,
p.60). They are followed by
persistent red berries in
autumn. 'Decorus' ♀ is
recommended. Cotoneasters
are very hardy, happy on all
soils including difficult ones
like clay and chalk. In mass
plantings, they can achieve
almost complete ground
cover. Prune, if necessary, just
after flowering in spring.
C. microphyllus ♀ has tiny
leaves but large fruits; wider
than it is tall, it is good for
covering banks or draping
over walls. *C. salicifolius* and
'Exburyensis' (see p.12) are
much taller (to 5m) and more
graceful, with large leaves.

ELAEAGNUS

Evergreen
elaeagnus are
reasonably
hardy, fast-
growing, and
suitable for most soils in sun
or shade. Up to 4m tall, they
form bold backgrounds for
other plants. They do not
need pruning, but can be
trimmed to shape and will
tolerate the cutting of stems
for flower arrangements.
Elaeagnus × *ebbingei* is more
often thought of as a foliage
plant as its small, yellowish-
cream flowers are hidden
amongst the leaves in autumn.
However, the insignificant
appearance of the flowers is
made up for by their intensely
sweet fragrance. Other
evergreen elaeagnus also have
attractive foliage. *E.* ×
ebbingei 'Limelight' (below)
has greenish-yellow splashes
in the centre of its leaves.
E. pungens 'Maculata' ♀ is
especially vigorous, with
leaves splashed with yellow
in the centre; 'Variegata'
and 'Dicksonii' have leaves
edged in yellow.

CHOISYA 'AZTEC PEARL' ♀

COTONEASTER CONSPICUUS

ELAEAGNUS × *EBBINGEI*
'LIMELIGHT'

ESCALLONIA

'Apple Blossom' (*below*) is one of the prettiest escallonias, shrubs mostly 2–3m high with an open arching habit, carrying small flowers along their stems. The leaves are glossy and aromatic in warm weather. For dark pink, almost red flowers look for *E. rubra* **'Crimson Spire'** ♀ (with more upright growth, also suitable for hedging); for white flowers, *E.* **'Iveyi'** ♀. They are only reasonably hardy but are excellent for seaside gardens in mild areas; they are highly resistant to salt spray. Inland and in cold areas they need winter protection, or to grow against a sunny wall. They prefer full sun in most soils, and once established are quite drought-tolerant. Some are a little ungainly, but can be pruned to improve their shape (*see p.33*). The flowers are mostly borne on the current season's growth, so old stems can be cut out after flowering or in very early spring.

GARRYA

An evergreen with handsome, leathery leaves, *Garrya elliptica* (*below*) bears a profusion of flowers in the form of long catkins in late winter. The male and female flowers are carried on different plants, those on male forms being more conspicuous. The best of these is **'James Roof'** ♀. Like many plants from California, garryas are not reliably hardy and need a sheltered spot in most areas. They are not fussy as to soil type, as long it is well-drained and reasonably fertile. Tolerant of atmospheric pollution and some exposure to salt winds, they also grow in some shade, flowering well, for instance, on a wall that receives only morning sun. Prune, if necessary, in early spring after flowering, but not too hard; rather than training garryas formally against a wall, tie them in loosely. Growing to 3–5m, they make good hedges, provided that you do not prune too formally.

GREVILLEA

One of the hardier grevilleas, **G. rosmarinifolia** ♀ (*below*) is still too tender for cold-climate inland gardens but a beautiful shrub for mild regions, in a sheltered spot or with protection from winter cold, or in a conservatory. It has narrow, needle-like grey-green leaves, complemented for many weeks in late spring and summer by spikes of cream to light crimson flowers, shaped a little like those of a honeysuckle. For richer red flower colour, look for **'Canberra Gem'** ♀. All grevilleas prefer a sunny site in well-drained soil that is not too limy. Growing up to 2m, and more in mild districts, they associate well with other plants liking dry conditions, such as callistemon, rosemary and cistus. Pruning is generally unnecessary. Grevillea leaves may be spine-tipped and can cause skin irritation, so site carefully in family gardens and wear gloves to handle.

ESCALLONIA **'APPLE BLOSSOM'** ♀

GARRYA ELLIPTICA

GREVILLEA ROSMARINIFOLIA ♀

HYPERICUM

Hypericums thrive in almost any soil, in full sun or partial shade and, since they flower on new wood in summer, can be pruned hard in late winter or after flowering in autumn. Almost all have yellow flowers; *H.* × *inodorum* 'Elstead' also bears brilliant salmon-red fruits at the tips of the shoots. 'Hidcote' ♥ (*below*) is a superb hardy plant, deservedly one of the most popular of flowering shrubs. Up to 2m wide and tall, it is semi-evergeen, more prone to losing its leaves in colder areas. It carries a profusion of golden-yellow saucer-shaped flowers throughout summer and well into autumn. *H. calycinum* is a dwarf, creeping shrub with similar flowers ideal for mass ground cover, although it can become a spreading nuisance. *H.* × *moserianum* 'Tricolor' is also low-growing but much less vigorous, up to about 75cm tall, with leaves edged in pink and cream.

ITEA

Itea ilicifolia ♥ (*below*) is a beautiful shrub, to 3m or more in height, with rather lax stems and leaves that are holly-like with small prickles. Its narrow, hanging flower clusters, borne in late summer, look rather like catkins, up to 30cm long and made up of tiny greenish-cream flowers that have a light honey-like fragrance. It grows well in full sun or partial shade, but like many originally Chinese plants, prefers conditions that are not too dry or too hot. You may prune it after flowering in the autumn or in early spring, but only to maintain the shape of the plant and to remove very old growth once the shrub matures. Not many other iteas are generally available, but there is a North American species, *I. virginica*, which must be grown in lime-free soil and whose flowers are more erect and conspicuous than those of *I. ilicifolia*.

MAHONIA

Handsome foliage shrubs year-round, mahonias come into their own in winter, with spires of whorled flower clusters, clear yellow and smelling of honey and lily-of-the-valley. During winter the glossy, spiny leaves also often have a rich reddish tone, especially in open sites. *M. aquifolium* (*below*) is one of the hardiest, but while it is often used as underplanting for woodland where it has to thrive on neglect, it enjoys being looked after. Improving the soil and using a general fertilizer really encourages good foliage and flowers. Up to 2m tall, like most mahonias it needs frequent pruning to maintain a good shape. It can be planted in sun or shade in any soil as long as it is not too wet. *M. japonica* ♥ and the hybrids *M.* × *media* 'Charity' ♥ (*see p.13*) and 'Underway' ♥ (*see p.23*) enjoy similar conditions but are not quite as hardy, and prefer moister, shadier situations.

HYPERICUM 'HIDCOTE' ♥

ITEA ILICIFOLIA ♥

MAHONIA AQUIFOLIUM

OSMANTHUS

Osmanthus delavayi ♀ *(below)* is a dense, bushy evergreen, up to 2m tall and 3m wide, with small leaves and clusters of small, tubular flowers in spring, which are highly fragrant – altogether, a lovely shrub for almost any soil, including chalk, as long as it is not too dry. The flowers are borne more freely in an open, sunny position, but it is quite happy in partial shade. It is extremely slow to establish in its first few years, so do not prune young plants unless absolutely necessary. Once mature it can be, though does not need to be, pruned after flowering to give it a more compact shape. Similar, but larger and hardier, is *O.* × *burkwoodii* ♀, though it is not as delicate and sweetly scented as *O. delavayi. O. heterophyllus* has the same type of flowers but more holly-like leaves, splashed with cream in **'Variegatus'** ♀.

OZOTHAMNUS

Ozothamnus ledifolius ♀ *(below)* forms a dense bush up to 1.5m tall, with small, succulent leaves, tightly undercurled, of an unusual khaki green, yellow on the undersides. The flowers are starry and greyish-white, borne in clusters at the stem tips and resembling those of tree heaths (*see p.59*). The scent of its flowers and foliage, especially noticeable in hot weather, is most peculiar; it could perhaps be described as a mixture of honey and warm strawberry jam. It can be grown in most soils and although fully hardy it prefers a hot, dry spot. A naturally compact shrub, it requires little or no pruning. *O. rosmarinifolius* is less hardy, but taller (to 3m), and has lovely greyish-green, rosemary-like foliage. **'Silver Jubilee'** ♀ has an especially beautiful silver sheen to its leaves, and looks very well in Mediterranean-style gardens and plantings.

PRUNUS

Evergreen prunus are large, robust, useful shrubs, tolerant of pruning, and thus popular as screening plants or informal hedging. Their leaves remain a good, dark green throughout winter; in spring, the branches are covered with erect spikes of white flowers. *P. laurocerasus* ♀, the cherry laurel, will grow to up to 6m tall in sun or shade, and is suited to any soil except shallow, poor chalk. Prune it after flowering, if necessary. If you are trying to keep hedges reasonably compact, you can also prune lightly in early spring and autumn. There is a dwarf form, **'Otto Luyken'** ♀ *(below)*, only 1m high and good *en masse* for shrubby ground cover, with branches ascending at oblique angles. *P. lusitanica* ♀ (Portuguese laurel) is even hardier and tolerates chalk. It can be pruned closely and often to produce topiary-like shapes, though this means losing the flowers.

OSMANTHUS DELAVAYI ♀

OZOTHAMNUS LEDIFOLIUS ♀

PRUNUS LAUROCERASUS 'OTTO LUYKEN' ♀

SKIMMIA

The male and female flowers of skimmias are usually borne on separate plants, and where both grow together, the females will develop red berries. They grow in most soils, in sun or shade. There are several types of *S. japonica*, all with white flowers, which in **'Fragrans'** ♀ are scented. **'Bronze Knight'** (*below*) is a male form, no more than 1.5m tall, with flower buds of deep bronze that form in clusters in winter. Set against female plants with red berries, they really brighten up winter gloom. **'Rubella'** ♀ is another fine male form. The subspecies *reevesiana* will flower and fruit if grown alone, since male and female flowers develop on the same plant, making it an excellent choice for a small garden or a tub (*see p.76*). *S.* × *confusa* 'Kew Green' ♀ is male, with scented cream flowers. Skimmias are naturally neat, but if long stems spoil the shape, cut them back well to within the bush.

SKIMMIA JAPONICA 'BRONZE KNIGHT'

ZENOBIA

Zenobia pulverulenta (*below*) is the only species, a spreading  shrub, to 2m tall, with thin, irregular arching stems. Both the shoots and leaves are covered in a white bloom which fades with age. It flowers in mid-summer, bearing dangling clusters of waxy white bells very similar to the flowers of lily-of-the-valley; they look especially pretty against the white bloom of the new growth. It grows best in neutral to acid conditions, disliking chalk and lime, and enjoys fertile, humus-rich soil, so add plenty of organic matter – especially leafmould – when planting, and it will tolerate quite dry spells in summer. It thrives in light shade, and gives a fresh summer look among spring flowering woodland shrubs, such as rhododendrons (*see p.58*). Prune after flowering to neaten its shape, if desired. It may lose its leaves in hard winters, but will survive.

ZENOBIA PULVERULENTA

MORE CHOICES

Calluna (*see p.56*)
Carpenteria (*see p.63*)
Ceanothus, some (*see p.63*)
Cistus (*see p.70*)
Daphne (*see p.53*)
Erica (*see p.56*)
Fatsia (*see p.64*)
Hebe (*see p.67*)
Kalmia (*see p.57*)
Lavandula (*see p.53*)
Leptospermum (*see p.68*)
Olearia (*see p.68*)
Phlomis (*see p.72*)
Pieris (*see p.59*)
Pyracantha (*see p.61*)
Rhododendron, most (*see p.58*)
Rosmarinus (*see p.72*)
Sarcococca (*see p.54*)
Senecio (*see p.76*)
Vaccinium (*see p.59*)
Vinca (*see p.65*)
Yucca (*see p.72*)

Abelia × *grandiflora* ♀
To 3m tall, with arching branches and weigela-like flowers (*see p.45*). Borderline hardy, for full sun and shelter.

× *Fatshedera*
Hybrid between *Fatsia* (*see p.64*) and *Hedera* (ivy); similar to fatsia, enjoying the same conditions. Pollution-tolerant; good for city gardens where there is not much light. To 2m tall and 3m wide.

Viburnum (*see also p.55*)
Evergreen viburnums include *V. davidii* ♀ (*see p.15*), to 1.5m tall, and, twice the size, *V. tinus* (laurustinus), both dense and bushy with white flower clusters in late spring and late winter respectively, and blue-black fruits. Hardy, for sun or shade.

SHRUBS FOR FRAGRANCE

CALYCANTHUS

Known as the Californian allspice, *Calycanthus occidentalis* (*below*) has large, handsome pointed leaves, green and smooth beneath, and grows up to 2m wide and high. It is a very hardy, sun-loving, deciduous shrub with conspicuous red-brown flowers in summer and early autumn. The flowers are spidery and have a curiously pleasant fragrance of ripe fruit, perhaps a pear or medlar, and the foliage when crushed has a sweet, spicy aroma that gives the plant its common name. As with many aromatic shrubs, the scent is stronger in full sun. It can be grown in any well-drained, fertile soil. An interesting shrub but not spectacular, it is best blended in with others; *Ceanothus* (*see p.60*) and *Carpenteria* (*p.63*) enjoy the same conditions.

CHIMONANTHUS

Chimonanthus praecox, or wintersweet, grows up to 2.5m tall, and is similar in its foliage to *Calycanthus* (*left*) which belongs to the same family. It has small, stemless, spidery and waxy cream flowers with a purple stain at the centre (*see p.10*), borne in winter on the leafless branches. They have a sweet, spicy fragrance. It needs a sheltered, sunny spot in cooler climates, otherwise flowers may not be produced. Although the flowers are borne in winter they will resist all but the hardest frosts. Wintersweet can be grown in any well-drained soil including chalk. There are two forms with finer flowers, **'Grandiflorus'** ♀ (*below*), with larger leaves, and **var. *luteus*** ♀, which flowers later in the winter, its outer petals of a clear light yellow.

CLETHRA

Known as the sweet pepper bush in its native North America, *Clethra alnifolia* grows more or less upright to 2.5m tall. Shoots bear terminal clusters of small, fragrant white flowers in late summer. **'Rosea'** has pink flowers. Another clethra from China, *C. barbinervis* ♀, enjoys the same kind of conditions. It is slightly more showy than *C. alnifolia*, but is more vulnerable to damage by late spring frosts.

Clethras prefer an acid soil that is moisture-retentive. They can be grown in quite wet ground if necessary, in full sun or partial shade. Since they flower in late summer on the current season's growth they can be hard-pruned in early spring, or you can simply deadhead the fading flowers and seedheads to encourage more vigour.

CALYANTHUS OCCIDENTALIS

CHIMONANTHUS PRAECOX '*GRANDIFLORUS*' ♀

CLETHRA ALNIFOLIA

DAPHNE

Several daphnes are intensely fragrant. Many are difficult to propagate and are therefore quite hard to come by. They can be fussy in the garden, too. Most enjoy good soil, including alkaline soil, that is moisture-retentive but well-drained, and should be grown in full sun to flower well. Do not prune unless absolutely necessary. **Daphne × burkwoodii** ♀ (see p.23), to 1.5m tall, is one of the easiest to grow, especially **'Somerset'** (below) and **'Carol Mackie'**, with variegated leaves. **D. bholua** is deciduous or semi-evergreen, up to 2m tall, with stout, erect branches bearing small clusters of exquisitely fragrant white flowers, pink-purple in bud, in late winter into early spring, depending on the climate. They are followed by black berries. **D. cneorum** is prostrate, with dark pink flowers. **D. collina**, **D. retusa** and **D. tangutica** ♀ are small evergreens.

DAPHNE × BURKWOODII 'SOMERSET'

HAMAMELIS

Hamamelis × intermedia 'Jelena' ♀ (below) is a superb winter-flowering witch hazel of spreading habit, over 3m high and up to 4m wide, with hazel-like leaves, and strongly fragrant yellow and coppery red flowers. The flowers, which have four thread-like petals, are completely frost-proof, appearing between mid-winter and early spring along the leafless twigs. The leaves often colour attractively in autumn. Witch hazels prefer acid to neutral soil with plenty of organic matter, and are very hardy. Although happy in full sun they are usually seen at their best in light woodland. Pruning is not usually necessary unless branches are badly misplaced, and is best done in early spring. If you prefer yellow flowers, perhaps the finest of all hamamelis is **'Pallida'** ♀ (see p.15) for the size and scent of its flowers and their light yellow colour.

HAMAMELIS × INTERMEDIA 'JELENA' ♀

LAVANDULA

Lavenders are wonderful small shrubs for mixing in borders or edging formal and herb beds. They grow well in containers, too (see p.76). The leaves are grey-green. Long stalks are topped by flower clusters in blues, mauves, white or pink in mid-summer. Regular light pruning is essential to keep lavenders bushy. Trim after flowering to remove flower stalks and clip over to the base of the last season's growth in early spring (see p.35). Pruning harder may kill older plants. Most are reasonably hardy, best in full sun in well-drained neutral or limy soils that do not dry out too much. **L. angustifolia** is the classic English lavender. **'Munstead'** is compact, while **'Hidcote'** ♀ is popular for its lovely dark flower colour, but is not very robust. **L. × intermedia 'Grappenhall'** is large and vigorous. French lavender, **L. stoechas** ♀ (see p.76), is not quite hardy.

LAVANDULA ANGUSTIFOLIA; 'NANA ALBA' IN FOREGROUND

LONICERA

Although many of the climbing honey-suckles are fragrant, only a few shrubby ones are. *L.* × *purpusii* is one of the best: a hybrid between *L. fragrantissima* (*below*) and *L. standishii*, it is free-flowering and vigorous. They are wide-spreading, graceful shrubs, up to 2m tall, which produce small, deliciously scented flowers in the depth of winter on their leafless branches. They can be grown in any well-drained, fertile soil in sun or partial shade. Other shrubby loniceras include *L. syringantha*, intricately branched, with small sea-green leaves and lilac-coloured flowers in spring. *L. tatarica* is not as heavily scented, but very hardy; '**Arnold's Red**' has rich pink flowers and red berries. Prune these winter- and spring-flowering honeysuckles after flowering, to shape and to remove old, unproductive wood.

PHILADELPHUS

The foliage of philadelphus, or mock orange, is rather ordinary, but their burst of white flowers in early or mid-summer, with a fragrance that carries over a wide area, makes them a must in any garden. They can be grown in most well-drained soils, even on poor chalk, in full sun or partial shade. As they have a tendency to get overgrown and woody, prune some old stems right to the ground each year, and if necessary, cut some flowered stems back to within a few centimetres of the old wood. There are many hybrids. '**Virginal**' ♀ (*below*), very hardy and up to 3m tall, has the scented, cup-like white flowers typical of most, but many-petalled. '**Belle Etoile**' ♀ (*see p.17*) has maroon blotches at the base of the petals; '**Minnesota Snowflake**' is very hardy. *P. coronarius* '**Aureus**' ♀ has golden foliage, best in shade; '**Variegatus**' ♀ has white-edged leaves.

SARCOCOCCA

Sarcococca confusa ♀ (*below*) is a typical Christmas box, an attractive small evergreen, to about 1m, with small creamy-white flowers in winter which, though almost hidden among the foliage, carry the sweetest and most pervasive fragrance. They are followed by black berries in late summer. The small, pointed glossy leaves make a neat bush, best grown in partial shade on any well-drained soil. The soil can be acid or limy and, once the plant is established, quite dry. Sometimes grown as informal low hedging, sarcococcas can be pruned in early spring to help maintain a good shape. They may not be fully hardy in very cold areas.

Other species have similar flowers. *S. hookeriana* ♀ has more upright, narrow growth although var. *humilis* is low-growing; '**Purple Stem**' has richly tinted young shoots. *S. ruscifolia* is taller but not as hardy.

LONICERA FRAGRANTISSIMA

PHILADELPHUS 'VIRGINAL' ♀

SARCOCOCCA CONFUSA ♀

SYRINGA

The common garden lilac, *S. vulgaris*, is a large shrub or even a small tree, growing up to 6m tall. The flowers are produced in dense sprays in spring, and are sweetly scented. Lilacs are hardy and happy in most soils, especially chalk, and flower best in full sun. Pruning consists of removing spent flowerheads and old wood immediately after flowering. You can also prune hard to a stump to renovate lilacs; regrowth is vigorous but there may be no flowers for a year or two. Flower colour ranges mostly from white and cream through classic mauves to red-purple. 'Madame Lemoine' ♥ (*below*), 'Katherine Havemeyer' ♥ (lavender-purple), 'Charles Joly' (dark purple-red) and 'Primrose' (pale yellow) are among the most popular. For the smaller garden try *S. × persica* ♥, *S. pubescens* subsp. *microphylla* or *S. meyeri* 'Palibin' ♥, often grown in containers (*see p.77*).

VIBURNUM

The fragrant viburnums are superb garden plants. *V. × bodnantense* 'Dawn' ♥ (*below*) is a fine, upright shrub that can flower from autumn to early spring. Growing up to 3m tall, the branches arch out when mature, and the old wood bears many small clusters of sweetly scented, rose-tinted flowers. The flower buds are remarkably frost hardy, but if damaged, more are produced. One of its parents, *V. farreri* ♥, is very similar, but has smaller flowers. *V. × burkwoodii* is semi-evergreen with shiny leaves and white flowerheads from pink buds in early spring. *V. carlesii*, *V. × juddii* ♥ and *V. bitchiuense* flower a little later, with a scent reminiscent of old-fashioned carnations. All are hardy, suitable for most fertile soils, in sun or partial shade. To prune, cut 2–3 old stems down to the base after flowering, to encourage new growth.

SYRINGA VULGARIS
'MADAME LEMOINE' ♥

VIBURNUM × BODNANTENSE
'DAWN' ♥

MORE CHOICES

FRAGRANT FLOWERS
Abelia × grandiflora ♥ (*see p.51*)
Berberis darwinii ♥, *B. × stenophylla* ♥ (*see p.46*)
Buddleja davidii (*see p.40*), or try the more unusual *B. globosa* ♥, a large shrub with spherical clusters of orange-yellow, honeyed flowers. Unlike *B. davidii*, it is not pruned hard.
Choisya ternata ♥ (*see p.47*)
Cytisus battandieri ♥, *C. × praecox* (*see p.71*)
Elaeagnus angustifolia (*see p.74*), *E. × ebbingei* (*see p.47*)
Erica arborea (*see p.59*)
Itea ilicifolia ♥ (*see p.49*)
Magnolia grandiflora (*see p.61*)
Mahonia (*see p.49*)
Osmanthus (*see p.50*)
Ozothamnus ledifolius ♥ (*see p.50*)
Perovskia atriplicifolia (*see p.72*)
Prunus mume (*see p.43*)
Rhododendron (*see p.58*): deciduous azaleas such as *R. luteum* ♥, *R. viscosum* ♥ and their hybrids, including the Exbury types; fragrant evergreens include the Loderi group, such as 'King George', and hybrids of *R. decorum*.
Ribes odoratum (*see p.44*)
Skimmia japonica 'Fragrans' ♥ (*see p.51*)
Spartium junceum ♥ (*see p.69*)

FRAGRANT FOLIAGE
Cistus ladanifer ♥, *C. × cyprius* ♥ (*see p.70*)
Escallonia (*see p.48*)
Rosmarinus officinalis (*see p.73*)
Santolina chamaecyparissus ♥ (*see p.73*)

SHRUBS FOR ACID SOIL

CALLUNA

Heather or ling, *Calluna vulgaris*, is a dense, evergreen, ground-covering dwarf shrub with small stems covered in tiny bell-flowers in late summer. Callunas prefer acid but well-drained, light soils. On rich soils they grow vigorously; on poorer soils they are more compact. Best in full sun, they are useful gap-fillers. In sandy soils, the stems, if buried, will root to stabilize banks and slopes. They grow well in containers. Old flowering stems may be trimmed after flowering, although some have seedheads and foliage that are attractive during winter; delay pruning these until early spring. There are hundreds to choose from, with white, pink or crimson flowers, and many with bright foliage: gold, silver or reddish-bronze. The latter are excellent providers of winter cheer.

CORYLOPSIS

The only corylopsis that really dislikes limy soils, *C. pauciflora* ♀ (*below*) is one of the best – densely branched, deciduous, up to 2m tall with slender stems, for semi-shade or light woodland. Its leaves are hazel-like, and pinky-red as they emerge in spring. The early spring flowers are catkin-like, a lovely primrose yellow and lightly fragrant. The flowers and young growth are prone to frost damage, although the plant itself is reasonably hardy. Young growth is also prone to scorch in hot sun. Pruning is unnecessary if plants have room for their graceful habit to develop. Other corylopsis tolerate some alkalinity, given deep soil. *C. glabrescens* and *C. sinensis* are broader-growing. *C. sinensis* 'Spring Purple' has coppery-purple young leaves.

ENKIANTHUS

Enkianthus campanulatus ♀ (*below*) is a distinctive, deciduous hardy shrub up to 3m tall, with upright branches and leaves arranged in whorls that take on exquisite colourings in autumn. A lovely plant to grow with other woodlanders like corylopsis, magnolias and camellias, it thrives in moisture-retentive, humus-rich soil, under trees or in full sun in cool regions. The flowers are bell-like, carried in drooping clusters on the previous season's growth in early summer amid emerging foliage. The flowers can vary from greenish-cream to rich bronze; although they are somewhat subdued in their colouring, their poise makes them curious and charming. Do not prune unless you need to remove old and dead wood, in which case, prune in early spring.

CALLUNA VULGARIS 'ANTHONY DAVIS' ♀

CORYLOPSIS PAUCIFLORA ♀

ENKIANTHUS CAMPANULATUS ♀

ERICA

Erica has given its name to the heath and heather family (Ericaceae) and familiarly to the group of plants that are acid-loving, or intolerant of alkaline soil (ericaceous). *Erica carnea* is the most familiar, a dwarf evergreen shrub with rosy-red flowers in late winter and early spring, forming dense hummocks and spreading mats. Best grown in full sun or partial shade in light, acid soils, it will tolerate neutral soil if you add plenty of leafmould or other organic matter. There are numerous heathers, two of the most popular being 'Springwood White' ♀ and 'Springwood Pink'. 'Vivellii' ♀ (*below*) is covered in vivid carmine flowers, with tiny green leaves turning a lovely bronze-red in winter. *Erica cinerea*, the bell heather, and *E. vagans* are also intolerant of limy soils. All make good underplanting for camellias and rhododendrons, and grow well in containers.

FOTHERGILLA

Fothergilla major ♀ (*below*) is a slow-growing, rounded shrub, to 2.5m tall, with rounded hazel-like leaves that turn to conspicuous red and yellow in autumn. Together with witch hazels (*Hamamelis*), which belong to the same family, they provide some of the best leaf colour in acid-soil gardens. With a combination of these, enkianthus and Japanese maples, the autumn garden can rival the spring garden for colour. Fothergilla bears white bottlebrush-like clusters of flowers just before the leaves emerge in spring. It is very hardy and prefers moist, peaty acid soil. As it naturally forms a well-shaped bush, no pruning should be necessary, except to remove any dead or diseased wood as the plant ages. *F. gardenii* is smaller, to only 1m high. Its flowers are similar but scented, and 'Blue Mist' has glaucous grey tints to its foliage.

KALMIA

The mountain laurel or calico bush can be 10m tall in its native North America, but *Kalmia latifolia* ♀ (*below*) normally grows to only 3–4m in northern Europe and other cool-summer regions. It has bold, laurel-like leaves topped in early summer by clusters of beautiful, star-shaped pink buds, almost like icing on a cake, that open to saucers of white with red spots. Slow sometimes to get established, kalmias enjoy full sun, but in areas with hot, bright summers they flower well in shade. They prefer rich, moisture-retentive soil, tolerating dry conditions only in late summer. They can be pruned after flowering to shape but otherwise need little attention. For stronger flower colour try 'Clementine Churchill', near-red; 'Freckles' has more pronounced spotting. *K. angustifolia* ♀ is smaller, to 1m, with narrow leaves and rosy-red flowers.

ERICA CARNEA 'VIVELLII' ♀

FOTHERGILLA MAJOR ♀

KALMIA LATIFOLIA ♀

RHODODENDRONS

A very large genus of plants, including those previously and still familiarly called azaleas. There are hundreds of species and thousands of hybrids, mostly evergreen, varying widely in size, but mostly of bushy habit.

In general they all prefer acid soils containing plenty of organic matter. They have a fibrous root system which benefits from a mulch of rotted leaves or peat substitute; do not use spent mushroom compost, which contains lime. A mulch also helps to conserve moisture, which the plants enjoy; *R. viscosum* ♀ will even grow in a swamp. Some will tolerate a reasonable amount of exposure to wind and full sun while others, particularly the large-leaved types, revel in the protective shade of deep-rooted trees. In areas with chalky or limy, alkaline soil, rhododendrons and azaleas can be grown in containers filled with an ericaceous (lime-free) compost mix.

Pruning needs vary. Most should not need pruning, but will flower better the following year if they are deadheaded (*see p.32*). Some, including

the Hardy Hybrids (*see below*), can be cut back hard if necessary after flowering. Azaleas can be clipped over after flowering. Some species of rhododendrons, especially those with smooth and peeling bark, may resent being pruned.

Evergreen rhododendrons

These include many choice and fussy collector's plants such as the blue-flowered *R. augustinii*, *R. auriculatum*, with heavenly, fragrant white blooms, and huge-leaved, cream-flowered *R. sinogrande* ♀. However, *R. catawbiense* and *R. ponticum* are both extremely tough species that have contributed to the group known as the **Hardy Hybrids**, with a vast range of flower colours: try rose-crimson 'Cynthia' ♀, dark crimson 'Lord Roberts', rosy 'Pink Pearl', or the rich purple of 'Purple Splendour' ♀. 'Mrs G.W. Leak' is pink with dark markings; 'Sappho' ♀ mauve in bud, opening white with dark throats.

Dwarf hybrids

Many of these originate from rock garden species like blue *R. impeditum* ♀ or pink *R. williamsianum* ♀. Most have

small leaves. 'Blue Diamond' (*below left*) is easy to grow, up to 1.5m tall. 'Elizabeth' (*below centre*) is a fine red with tiered branches. The white *R. yakushimanum*, with white-felted young growth, has given rise to a race of new and very hardy dwarf hybrids (*see p.77 for recommendations*), perfectly rounded shrubs, mostly white-flowered, pink in bud.

Deciduous azaleas

Beautiful plants, often scented and with fine autumn leaf colour. *R. luteum* ♀ has yellow flowers; those of *R. molle* are orange-red, and *R. viscosum* ♀, pink-tinged white. There are many hybrid groups between them, such as the **Exbury** and **Ghent** hybrids, characterized by big clusters of large flowers.

Evergreen azaleas

Very popular and versatile, these include potted house plants, and in the garden can be used singly or in mass plantings, smothered with flowers. They are excellent shrubs for containers (*see p.77 for recommendations*).

RHODODENDRON 'BLUE DIAMOND'

RHODODENDRON 'ELIZABETH'

RHODODENDRON 'SAPPHO' ♀

PIERIS

Pieris japonica is a hardy evergreen with a dense habit and very attractive, dark, narrow leaves. Especially beautiful is 'Variegata', with cream-edged leaves; a smaller pieris, it is good in containers (see also p.76). The lily-of-the-valley-like flower sprays, usually white but pink in the hybrid P. 'Flamingo', form in autumn and then open either in late winter or early spring depending on the weather. The foliage and flowers are vulnerable to late spring frosts so, although the plant itself is hardy, it should be planted in shelter from cold winds and out of frost pockets. Pieris prefer acid soils containing plenty of organic matter, in full sun or partial shade. Some have bright red young foliage, such as 'Forest Flame' ♀ (see p.16), or P. formosa var. forrestii 'Wakehurst' ♀. This is less hardy than P. japonica, which has attractive, pinkish young growth.

PIERIS FORMOSA VAR. FORRESTII

VACCINIUM

The cowberry, V. vitis-idaea, (below) is the most popular vaccinium, for the garden, a dwarf ever-green with a creeping, mat-forming habit. The small box-like leaves are dark, glossy green above and paler beneath. The flowers are held in terminal sprays of tiny white bells in early summer, followed by dark red berries in autumn. Vacciniums also include many popular fruiting shrubs, such as blueberry, cranberry, bilberry and huckleberry. They mostly prefer moist, acid soil, some liking highly acid and very wet conditions, as in a peat bog. They tolerate some shade. They need little pruning except for the highbush blueberry, V. corymbosum ♀, a deciduous shrub with fine autumn colour that is often trained on a short, clear trunk to make a bush. Pruning can be carried out after flowering, but avoid cutting away any potential fruit.

VACCINIUM VITIS-IDAEA SUBSP. MINUS

MORE CHOICES

Amelanchier (see p.66)
Clethra (see p.52)
Colutea arborescens (see p.67)
Fatsia japonica ♀ (see p.64)
Hamamelis (see p.53)
Hydrangea macrophylla, H. quercifolia ♀ (see pp.42, 64)
Magnolia many (see p.61)
Skimmia (see p.51)

Erica arborea
The tree heath is similar-looking in its foliage and flowers to other ericas (see p.57) but on a much bigger scale, growing up to 6m tall and developing thick, woody branches. Its white spring flowers are borne in fragrant cones on green, upright shoots. Unlike small heathers, tree heaths can be cut very hard back if necessary, after flowering.

Arctostaphylos uva-ursi
The red bearberry, closely related to Vaccinium (left), is another very low-growing evergreen that makes effective ground cover even in very sandy dry soils. It has small white flowers and red berries.

The following tolerate acid soils if the pH value is above 5.5:
Cotoneaster (see pp.47, 60)
Cytisus (see p.71)
Elaeagnus (see p.47)
Hypericum (see p.49)
Philadelphus (see p.54)
Pyracantha (see p.61)
Syringa (see p.55)
Viburnum (see pp.45, 55)
Weigela (see p.45)

SHRUBS FOR WALL-TRAINING

CEANOTHUS

Normally growing up to 3-4m, evergreen ceanothus (Californian lilac) are either upright or prostrate shrubs, mainly blue-flowered and among the finest wall shrubs for areas that do not suffer from harsh winters. The small evergreen leaves are held close to the stems; above them are carried small, dense balls of tiny flowers, of an especially rich dark blue in 'Concha' (*below*). Other good blue ceanothus include *C.* × *veitchianus*, 'Trewithen Blue' ♔, 'Millerton Point', 'Yankee Point' and 'Cascade' ♔; for white flowers, choose 'Snow Flurries'. If grown untrained they need plenty of room and stout supports to hold their weight. Prune after flowering, cutting back flowered shoots no thicker than a pencil. Do not prune back into old bare wood; it will not reshoot.

CHAENOMELES

Familiarly known as japonicas, these are popular wall shrubs for even the coldest gardens. *C. speciosa* types, vigorous shrubs up to 2.5m tall, are the most suitable for training. The species is red-flowered, with small cup-shaped flowers in late winter and early spring but there are other colours; in 'Moerloosei' ♔ (often labelled as 'Apple Blossom') they are especially pretty, white on the outside and deep pink inside. The flowers are carried on the previous season's growth. Prune wall-trained plants twice a year to encourage the build-up of flowering spurs (*see p.37*) close to the main branches, close to the wall. First shorten the long summer shoots by two-thirds in mid-summer, then shorten these growths again in late winter to three or four buds.

COTONEASTER

Small-leaved cotoneasters that carry their branches in flat fan arrangements or "fishbone" shapes, for example *C. horizontalis* ♔ and *C. divaricatus* (*below and p.21*), make low-growing shrubs, often used as a ground cover, but are also excellent for wall-training in sun or shade, in any climate and most soils. They need very little pruning, simply encouragement, guiding stems to supports, to grow flat up against a wall, where they can reach up to 2–3m. The small white flowers open from pink buds in spring and are followed by red berries in autumn which can persist well into winter: a fine sight among the leaves as they turn red in autumn. Pruning can be carried out after flowering or in late winter but should rarely be necessary.

CEANOTHUS 'CONCHA'

CHAENOMELES SPECIOSA 'MOERLOOSEI' ♔

COTONEASTER DIVARICATUS

MAGNOLIA

Magnolia grandiflora is not as slow to grow and flower as some other magnolias. In some parts of the world this magnificent evergreen can reach tree-like proportions, but in most gardens it is grown as a large shrub or trained against a house wall, where in cold areas it benefits from the shelter and extra warmth. The flowers in late summer and autumn are spectacular: large, creamy-white, with a hypnotic fragrance; a single one can scent an entire room. It has handsome, large, shiny green leaves, shorter and broader in **'Goliath'** ♀ (*below*) and narrower in **'Exmouth'** ♀; **'Ferruginea'** has more rusty hairiness under the leaf. *M.* **'Maryland'**, a hybrid, has slightly smaller flowers but is hardier. All are happy in almost any soil, including fairly limy ones, as long as it is deep and fertile. Prune in early spring or autumn to train to the wall (*see p.37*).

MAGNOLIA GRANDIFLORA 'GOLIATH' ♀

PYRACANTHA

Easily grown in most soil types, in sun or shade, pyracanthas are very useful shrubs for wall-training, as they can be pruned to keep a dense habit and still flower well; this also makes them very suitable for intruder-proof flowering hedging. Deciduous, with sharply thorny stems and bunches of brilliantly coloured berries in autumn, they are also known as firethorns. They bear clusters of white flowers in spring. They are large shrubs, up to 5m tall when freestanding, that need sturdy support for wall-training, such as a frame of wooden battens. The young stems are flexible and can be trained horizontally to go around windows and doors. *P.* **'Watereri'** ♀ (*below*) is compact and recommended for walls, as are *P.* **rogersiana** ♀ with orange fruits (yellow in **'Flava'** ♀); **'Teton'**, with an erect habit and orange fruits, and **'Sparkler'**, with cream leaf margins.

PYRACANTHA 'WATERERI' ♀

MORE CHOICES

Other shrubs for wall-training, many of which will appreciate the extra shelter of the wall in cold climates, include:

Chimonanthus (*see p.52*)
Cotoneaster conspicuus **'Decorus'** ♀, *C. microphyllus* ♀ (*see p.48*) Will need regular clipping to keep them flat and dense. The large-leaved types such as *C.* × *watereri* are not suitable.
Forsythia suspensa ♀ (*see p.41*)
Fuchsia magellanica (*see p.41*)
Garrya (*see p.48*)
Itea ilicifolia ♀ (*see p.49*)
Olearia macrodonta ♀ (*see p.68*)
Prunus cistena, P. mume, P. triloba (*see p.43*)
Stachyurus (*see p.65*); **'Magpie'** is especially pretty wall-trained
Viburnum macrocephalum (*see p.45*)

Alternatives to *Buddleja davidii* (*see p.40*) ideal for walls, similar-looking but less hardy and more delicate in flower and leaf, are *Buddleja crispa*, up to 2m tall, with heavily white-felted stems and leaves and purply-pink flowers, ideal as a backdrop to a white or silver planting scheme; and *Buddleja* × *colvilei* **'Kewensis'**, a much larger shrub up to 4m tall, with large drooping spires of fragrant, pinky-red flowers in spring. Both prefer a sunny position in well-drained soil. Unlike *B. davidii* they should not be hard-pruned; prune *B. crispa* lightly in early spring, and 'Kewensis' after flowering.

WALL SHRUBS FOR MILD AREAS

ABUTILON

Not hardy where winters are cold, abutilons can be grown as free-standing shrubs elsewhere, but their slender stems make them prone to flopping over, and tying them into a wired wall gives them support as well as providing shelter and reflected warmth where needed. *A. megapotamicum* ♥ (*below*), up to 2.5m tall, has small, arrow-shaped, dark green leaves, marked with cream in '**Variegatum**'. It needs moisture-retentive soil in full sun. In mild areas the flowers can be carried at almost any time of year but mostly during summer and autumn. Although the flowers are not large individually, the quantity of contrasting red and yellow blooms makes a striking and intriguing display. You can prune in early spring, cutting hard back to the wall, if necessary, or to tidy the plant.

AZARA

Azara integrifolia (*below*) is a tall evergreen shrub which in cool climates can be grown against a wall for protection. *A. microphylla* ♥ is hardier, to 3 or 4m tall, with very small leaves and a stiff upright habit. Both this and *A. integrifolia* have good variegated-leaved forms; all have yellow flowers. The leaves are oval and dark green. The flowers are little tassels of yellow stamens borne in early spring, sweetly fragrant. Azaras tend to form a strong central stem, almost like a small tree, but can be pruned to maintain a denser habit. They can be grown on most soils that are free-draining, and are fairly drought-tolerant when established, so cope well in the rain shadow created by a wall or fence, provided that they have been well cared for when young.

CARPENTERIA

Known as the Californian orange blossom, *Carpenteria californica* ♥ (*below*) is a rounded evergreen shrub, hardy only in warm districts. The foliage needs not only the warmth of a wall but additional shelter from cold winds, to stop it becoming bruised and unsightly. The flowers resemble those of its close relative, *Philadelphus*, carried in clusters during summer. Look out for plants with names such as '**Ladhams' Variety**', which have reliably good, large flowers. Carpenterias also have attractive peeling bark. Grow them free-standing (to about 5m tall) or loosely tied in against a wall, in almost any well-drained soil; they thrive in sun. Prune lightly after flowering or harder, if needed, in spring; this may be at the expense of some flowers.

ABUTILON MEGAPOTAMICUM ♥

AZARA INTEGRIFOLIA

CARPENTERIA CALIFORNICA ♥

CORONILLA

Known as the scorpion senna, *Coronilla emerus* (*below*), sometimes also called *Hippocrepis*, is a sun-loving, deciduous member of the pea family that needs a sheltered site. Its leaves are divided into tiny round leaflets, and throughout the summer it is covered with small yellow pea-flowers, tipped with a touch of rusty red. Long, slender seedpods then develop, curved like a scorpion's tail. Up to 2m tall and wide, forming a dense thicket of a bush, it can be tied in loosely to a wall to draw it up in height and make it more compact, as well as giving extra warmth. It responds well to pruning, in early spring, to keep it in shape. In mild climates choose the more attractive but more tender *C. valentina* 'Variegata' has lovely blue-green leaves edged in cream. Much smaller, it could be grown in a pot and overwintered under cover.

CORONILLA EMERUS

FREMONTODENDRON

Evergreen, or often semi-evergreen, fast-growing shrubs for sheltered and warm gardens, fremonodendrons are easy to train against walls, although you must wear gloves when handling them: the hairs on the stems and leaves irritate some people's skin. They also shed these hairs freely, so beware when gardening beneath them. 'California Glory' ♀ (*below*) is the most widely seen; it is a spectacular shrub when in full flower, up to 7m tall, covered in large, yellow cup-shaped flowers from early summer through autumn. Fremontodendrons are not fussy as to soil type, as long as it it free-draining. They do not like being transplanted, however, and it is best to plant a small specimen; once established, it will grow away rapidly. Prune the shoot tips to encourage a more bushy habit and to keep the shrub close to the wall.

FREMONTODENDRON
'CALIFORNIA GLORY' ♀

MORE CHOICES

These shrubs are also only for mild and warm-climate regions, unless they can be given a very favourable spot, such as a sunny house wall or courtyard garden. In cool climates they make good conservatory plants.

Callistemon (see p.46)
Grevillea (see p.48)

Acacia dealbata ♀
Best in warm-climate gardens, where it can grow into a 30m-tall tree, but worth trying with the protection of a wall in mild districts. The fluffy sprays of tiny yellow flowers in early spring are very fragrant. Even where they are not reliably produced, the shrub is beautiful for its feathery, grey-blue foliage alone. *A. baileyana* ♀ is smaller, of similar hardiness; its foliage has a slight purple tinge to it.

Piptanthus nepalensis
A semi-evergreen, vigorous shrub up to 4m tall, with three-lobed dark green leaves and spikes of bright yellow pea-flowers in early summer. Grown in full sun in any fertile soil, it thrives in milder climates or with the protection of a wall. Flowering on the previous season's growth, it should be pruned after flowering.

Plumbago auriculata ♀
Sprawling deciduous shrub that needs support, with showers of lovely pale blue flowers throughout summer. Against a wall, it may reach 4–5m; in a container in full sun, about 1m. Prune in early spring to encourage new growth. The variety **alba** is white-flowered.

SHRUBS FOR SHADE

CAMELLIA

Camellia × williamsii is a hybrid with many good qualities. It is hardier than *C. japonica* (*see p.46*), but with smaller evergreen leaves that are more pointed. Its habit is more lax, and the flowers are produced over a longer season. The flower buds are vulnerable to late frosts, so in cold climates a shady position is ideal, to protect them from too-rapid thawing in early morning sun. In mild years, blooms may open in early winter and sporadically until spring. In colder winters they flower mostly in early spring. All camellias prefer an acid soil with plenty of organic matter, such as leafmould, added. In dappled shade or against a wall they can reach up to 3m. Among the finest are **'Donation'** ♥ (silver-pink, semi-double flowers), **'J.C. Williams'** ♥ (pale pink) and **'Francis Hanger'** (*below*).

CAMELLIA × WILLIAMSII
'FRANCIS HANGER'

FATSIA

Grown chiefly for its leathery, deeply lobed, large evergreen leaves, *Fatsia japonica* ♥, a relative of the common ivy, has ivy-like, greenish-cream "drumstick" flowerheads in autumn (*below*). These are often damaged by frosts, but if they develop unscathed, large bunches of black berries develop. Needing some shelter for its large leaves, fatsia thrives in most soils and, like ivy, in quite heavy shade, reaching up to 3m. The great quality of this shrub is that of evoking a tropical or sub-tropical effect, combining well with plants such as bamboo and tree ferns, which also do well in sheltered moist shade. **'Variegata'** ♥ has creamy-white splashes on the leaves. If fatsias grow too large they can be pruned as hard as you like, in early spring before the new shoots emerge.

FATSIA JAPONICA ♥

HYDRANGEA

All hydrangeas (*see also p.42*) will grow in shade, but some are especially suited to it. *H. aspera* is one of these, and the lovely **Villosa Group** ♥ (*below*) has the best flowers, plus long, velvety leaves and peeling, grey-brown papery bark. The large flowerheads have a ring of lacy, rose-lilac florets surrounding a boss of minute, rich blue flowers. Unlike other hydrangeas, if flower buds are damaged by late spring frosts, more shoots grow to put on the late summer show. It is happy in any rich, cool soil, in the dappled shade of trees or shaded by a building, growing up to 4m tall and often much wider. It can be pruned in late winter, quite hard if needed. For a smaller shrub, shade-loving *H. quercifolia* ♥ grows to about 2m tall, with cones of white florets and oak-like leaves that take on good autumn colour.

HYDRANGEA ASPERA
VILLOSA GROUP ♥

STACHYURUS

Stachyurus praecox ℗ (*below*) is an elegant, fairly upright deciduous shrub, to 2.5m tall, with deep wine-red stems that contrast perfectly with the small, rounded, pale yellow flowers that hang in catkins off the leafless stems in late winter. Stachyurus will grow on any lime-free soil, but if there is plenty of organic matter in it they tolerate more alkaline conditions. They are best grown in shade where the early flowers and leaves will be more protected from frost. Pruning is usually unnecessary unless a branch spoils the shape or becomes very old and unproductive. The best time to prune is in early spring after flowering. *S. chinensis* differs little from *S. praecox* except that its stems are not red-tinted, and it has slightly longer flower tassels. The beautiful, variegated **'Magpie'** has leaves splashed creamy white with pink around their margins.

STACHYURUS PRAECOX ℗

VINCA

Periwinkles, which give their name to the piercing blue of their flowers, are trailing evergreen shrubs that form a ground-covering carpet by means of spreading roots and arching stems which root as they touch the ground. Flowers open along the stems during spring and early summer, with a few carried on into the autumn. The greater periwinkle, *V. major*, can be very invasive, even in its variegated form, but *V. minor*, the lesser periwinkle (*below*), is a useful plant for shade in most soil types, and will, once established, tolerate quite dry conditions. Although it grows in heavy shade, it flowers best in dappled shade. Every few years it is worth cutting the whole plant down to the ground to encourage fresh new growth. This is best done after the first flush of flowers in spring. There are periwinkles with variegated leaves and with white, pink or double flowers.

VINCA MINOR

MORE CHOICES

Chaenomeles (see p.40)
Choisya (see p.75)
Corylopsis (see p.56)
Cotoneaster (see pp.47, 60)
Daphne, especially evergreens such as
  D. *laureola (see p.53)*
Deutzia (see p.40)
Elaeagnus × ebbingei,
  E. *pungens (see p.47)*
Enkianthus (see p.56)
Erica (see p.56)
Forsythia (see p.41)
Fothergilla (see p.48)
Garrya (see p.48)
Hamamelis (see p.53)
Hypericum (see p.49)
Kalmia (see p.57)
Kerria japonica (see p.42)
Magnolia (see p.61)
Mahonia (see p.49)
Nandina domestica ℗
  (see p.45)
Osmanthus delavayi ℗,
  O. *× burkwoodii*,
  O. *heterophyllus*
  (see p.50)
Pieris (see p.59)
Philadelphus (see p.54)
Pyracantha (see p.61)
Rhododendrons and azaleas
  (see p.58)
Ribes sanguineum,
  R. *odoratum (see p.44)*
Sarcococca (see p.54)
Skimmia (see p.51)
Vaccinium (see p.59)
Viburnum × burkwoodii,
  V. *carlesii (see p.55)*,
  V. *davidii* ℗ *(see p.51)*
Weigela (see p.45)

SHRUBS FOR EXPOSED SITES

AMELANCHIER

Amelanchier canadensis (*below*) is a large deciduous shrub, sometimes a small tree, with beautiful young foliage which unfurls with a pinkish tinge very early in the spring, at the same time as clusters of white flowers open. Often trained with a single trunk, it actually grows naturally as a multi-stemmed shrub. It can reach 6–7m in height. In autumn, the foliage takes on lovely, clear shades of red and pink.

Amelanchiers thrive in most soils that are not too limy and, although growing well in well-drained soil, tolerate almost bog-like conditions. Although they suit woodland they also grow well in very exposed situations and can withstand salt-laden winds. Pruning to shape, if necessary, and to remove old or dead wood is best carried out in late winter.

BERBERIS

B. thunbergii ♀ and its many forms are easy to grow in almost all soils, in full sun, except for **'Aurea'**, whose golden foliage tends to burn in hot sun. They are dense, very thorny, rounded shrubs with small leaves. The early summer flowers are pale yellow, hanging in small clusters, followed by bright red berries in autumn. The form **atropurpurea** (*below*) has dark coppery-purple leaves that turn wine-red in autumn. Some varieties have been bred for a compact or upright habit, ideal for hedges – either low for borders, or up to 2.5m tall for impenetrable boundary screens, useful to protect other plants in cold windy sites. Pruning can be difficult due to the thorns, but hard-pruning and shearing may be carried out in late winter and after flowering.

BRACHYGLOTTIS

'Sunshine' ♀ (*below*) is a very popular "ever-grey" shrub with silvery leaves, forming a dense mound up to 1m high and more across. Bright yellow flowers open from clusters of silvery-white buds; when in full flower the shrub is quite spectacular. **B. monroi** ♀ has smaller, wavy-edged leaves, not as silver, but is equally good in flower. Like many silver-leaved plants, they prefer full sun in well-drained soil. They are not hardy in cold areas but tolerate mild winds and sea spray. They make good companions for olearias (*overleaf*) and hebes (*facing page*) which enjoy similar conditions. Pruning simply consists of removing spent flowerheads to encourage a compact habit. Old or untrimmed straggly plants that have opened up can be hard-pruned after flowering.

AMELANCHIER CANADENSIS

BERBERIS THUNBERGII F. *ATROPURPUREA*

BRACHYGLOTTIS 'SUNSHINE' ♀

COLUTEA

Colutea arborescens is a quick-growing shrub, to 3m tall and wide, with divided leaves on grey shoots and warm yellow flowers throughout the summer. These are followed by inflated seedpods that give it its common name of bladder senna (senna being a name common to yellow-flowered members of the pea family). Ideal for poor, hungry soils, on dry sunny banks and even in polluted areas, it is hardy and takes considerable wind exposure. It can become untidy, but can be hard pruned in early spring, removing old and dead growth at the same time. Hybrids between this species and *C. orientalis*, with brownish-red flowers but otherwise similar, include *C. × media* 'Copper Beauty', with unusual coppery flowers. Good companions for colutea include dry soil-loving *Cytisus* and *Cistus* (*pp.70–71*) *Genista* (*right*) and *Tamarix* (*overleaf*).

GENISTA

Genista is very similar to *Cytisus* (*see p.71*) in many respects; both are known as brooms and prefer a sunny spot in dry areas. Many genistas, especially the low-growing types, will take considerable exposure even to salt-laden winds. They can be grown in most soil types and are fairly lime-tolerant. The only pruning that may be necessary is to trim over with shears after flowering to maintain a compact habit. Genistas are often rather short-lived. *G. pilosa* 'Procumbens' (*below*) is a dense, ground-hugging shrub forming a mat of grey-green stems, smothered with small golden-yellow flowers in early summer. Other prostrate brooms include *G. tinctoria* and double-flowered 'Flore Pleno' ♥. *G. lydia* ♥ grows a little taller. *G. hispanica* is the toughest, prickly and dense, similar to gorse. More tree-like and less hardy is *G. aetnensis* ♥, the Mount Etna broom.

HEBE

Hebes, almost all from New Zealand, are wind-resistant (including salt winds) but are not fully hardy in cold districts. They prefer full sun and thrive in any reasonable, well-drained soil, but although tolerating quite dry conditions, they are not drought-resistant. Pruning is usually unnecessary, but if you have to, always cut stems back to a leafy shoot, not into bare wood. *H. pinguifolia* 'Pagei' ♥ is one of the hardiest, and excellent ground cover. *H. albicans* ♥ (*see p.75*) and purple-tinged 'Red Edge' are slightly taller. The larger-leaved hebes are less hardy but more showy in flower; look for *H.* 'Midsummer Beauty' ♥, with long blue flower spikes and long leaves, 'Great Orme' ♥ (*see p.24*) and 'Amy', also called 'Purple Queen', up to 1.5m tall, with a purplish hue to the leaves harmonizing with the spikes of rosy-purple flowers in mid-summer.

COLUTEA ARBORESCENS

GENISTA PILOSA 'PROCUMBENS'

HEBE 'AMY'

HIPPOPHAE

Although not a showy flowerer, *Hippophae rhamnoides* ♀ (*below*), a tall, deciduous spiny shrub, has beautiful small, narrow grey leaves, scaly bark, tiny yellow-green flowers in spring and, on female plants, bright orange-yellow berries in autumn that may persist through the winter. It grows up to 4m tall. Its greatest assets are its tolerance to wind, especially salt winds, and its ability to grow in almost any soil, from very dry to almost boggy. Since on hippophaes, male and female flowers are carried on separate plants, it is necessary to plant at least one male plant for two or more females to ensure berry production, so these shrubs are ideal for group plantings and shelter hedges. Prune in late winter if necessary to improve the shape, which can become a little ungainly and leggy, cutting back as hard as you like.

LEPTOSPERMUM

Leptospermum lanigerum ♀ (*below*) is a beautiful, grey-leaved evergreen shrub native to Australia, where it can grow to 4m tall, flowering in early summer with groups of small white flowers with deep purple markings inside them. These nestle among young foliage that is silky and hairy on drooping branches, giving the whole plant an airy grace. Leptospermums prefer well-drained, acid to neutral soil in full sun, and will tolerate salt winds and an open position in milder areas. Though none is fully hardy, *L. lanigerum* is hardier than most and well worth trying. *L. scoparium*, smaller with green leaves, is more frequently grown but less hardy; look for 'Red Damask' ♀, which has long-lasting, double red flowers. In cool climates they will require the shelter of a wall. Prune to shape, if desired, in early spring.

OLEARIA

Olearias are medium-sized evergreens, smothered with white daisy-like flowers in early summer. The leaves, small and grey-felted, are soft to touch and aromatic. Olearias are best grown in full sun in any well-drained soil, and will even thrive on chalk. Although its parents are from Australasia, *O. × scilloniensis* ♀ (*below*) is from the Scilly Isles, where it has to tolerate very strong salt-laden winds. It is, however, not hardy in cold areas. The hardiest olearia is *O. × haastii*, which forms a dense hummock, bearing starry white flowers in late summer. Very tolerant of pruning (in early spring), olearias make ideal hedges and small windbreaks in maritime areas. The larger, holly-leaved *O. macrodonta* ♀, with grey-green leaves, can reach up to 4m and is ideal for this purpose, while *O. × haastii* would make a good low hedge.

HIPPOPHAE RHAMNOIDES ♀

LEPTOSPERMUM LANIGERUM ♀

OLEARIA × SCILLONIENSIS ♀

SPARTIUM

Closely related to both *Cytisus* and *Genista* (*see pp.71, 67*), and known as Spanish broom, **Spartium junceum** ♀ (*below*) is a Mediterranean shrub, strong-growing, often leggy in habit, up to 3m tall, with erect, slender stems and such small leaves as to look almost leafless. The flowers are typical of a broom: large, pea-like and yellow, and borne in terminal clusters in late summer and into autumn, with a wonderfully sweet fragrance. Spanish broom is easily grown and trouble-free, given a sunny position in any well-drained soil, even poor soil. Not fully hardy in cold inland areas, where it can be given the shelter of a wall, it is ideal for mild maritime regions, where its growth is more compact, being kept low and bushy by the sea winds. Like most brooms, it is best trimmed over in early spring with shears to stop it becoming too straggly.

SPARTIUM JUNCEUM ♀

TAMARIX

Reasonably hardy and easily grown in any soil type except shallow chalk, tamarisks are excellent plants for windy areas, particularly near the sea, where they happily tolerate salt winds. *T. ramosissima* (*below* and *p.25*) is a striking shrub for late summer, with feathery, pale grey-green foliage and large, soft pink airy plumes of flowers that branch and open for many weeks. It looks good growing among or behind tall perennials. Left unpruned it will form an almost tree-like shape, often leaning with a lop-sided look. It can also be hard-pruned in early spring to encourage larger flowers and a longer display. *T. tetrandra* ♀ and *T. parviflora* both flower in early summer, so hard pruning in spring would mean the loss of flowers. The best treatment for these is to prune lightly in summer after flowering, and again in winter.

TAMARIX RAMOSISSIMA

MORE CHOICES

FOR COLD, WINDY GARDENS
Calluna (*see p.56*)
Chaenomeles (*see p.40*)
Erica (*see p.56*)
Kerria japonica (*see p.42*)
Hydrangea paniculata (*see p.42*)
Kalmia (*see p.57*)
Rhododendron Hardy Hybrids and hybrids of *R. yakushimanum* (*see p.58*)
Spiraea × *vanhouttei* (*see p.44*)
Syringa vulgaris (*see p.55*)
Vaccinium some (*see p.59*)
Viburnum opulus, *V. dentatum* (*see p.45*)

FOR SEASIDE GARDENS
Buddleja davidii, *B. globosa* ♀ (*see pp.40, 55*)
Berberis darwinii ♀ (*see p.46*)
Calluna (*see p.56*)
Cistus ladanifer ♀ (*see p.70*)
Cotoneaster, all small-leaved types (*see pp.47, 60–61*)
Elaeagnus (*see pp.47, 74*)
Escallonia (*see p.48*)
Fuchsia magellanica (*see p.41*)
Hydrangea macrophylla (*see p.42*)
Lavandula (*see p.53*)
Phlomis (*see p.72*)
Prunus × *cistena* ♀, *P. maritima* (*see p.43*), also *P. spinosa*
Rosmarinus (*see p.72*)
Santolina (*see p.72*)
Viburnum opulus (*see p.45*)
Yucca (*see p.72*)

SHRUBS FOR DRY PLACES

CARYOPTERIS

Caryopteris × *clandonensis* (*below*) is a small, deciduous shrub, to 1.5m, with aromatic grey-green leaves and little clusters of bright blue flowers in late summer at the tips of stems and in the leaf joints. It blends well with late-flowering perennials and other small grey-leaved shrubs like lavender and perovskia. Best grown in a sunny site in any well-drained soil, caryopteris are reasonably hardy and once established tolerate quite dry conditions. Like other late-flowering shrubs they can be hard-pruned in spring: cut stems down to just above new, emerging shoots. **'Heavenly Blue'** ♥, **'Kew Blue'** and **'Ferndown'** (*see p.12*) vary in the intensity of blue but all are to be recommended. **'Worcester Gold'** has yellow-green leaves which contrast strikingly with the blue flowers.

CARYOPTERIS × CLANDONENSIS

CERATOSTIGMA

Ceratostigma flowers are of such a true blue, nearly cobalt, that they show up other so-called blue-flowered plants and are best planted among pinks and purples. *C. willmottianum* ♥ (*below*) is deciduous, up to 1m tall, flowering in late summer and into autumn. The leaves take on rich reddish autumn tints, showing off late flowers to even better advantage. Reasonably hardy, in full sun in well-drained soil it becomes quite drought-resistant. It may be cut down by winter frost, but you can prune down to new growth in early spring. This also encourages better flowers. *C. griffithii* is evergreen, denser, more bristly but not as hardy or showy. *C. plumbaginoides* ♥ is hardier, ground-covering and tolerant of dry shade beneath shrubs, with flame-coloured foliage in autumn.

CERATOSTIGMA WILLMOTTIANUM ♥

CISTUS

The sun or rock roses are small evergreens, up to 1.5m tall, with greyish foliage and large, wrinkled, papery-looking flowers. Many have blotches on the petals, such as *C.* × *purpureus* ♥ (*below*). *C. laurifolius* ♥ has larger, aromatic leaves and white flowers. Mostly native to Mediterranean regions, cistus are sun-lovers for dry soils of most types, including chalk. They are not suitable for cold gardens unless given some protection. *C.* × *corbariensis* ♥, with white flowers, is perhaps the hardiest. In general they dislike pruning, but can be trimmed lightly in early spring, back to new growth, to maintain well-formed bushes. Some, particularly hybrids of *C. ladanifer* ♥, can be leggy; tip-pruning growing shoots can help.

CISTUS × PURPUREUS ♥

CYTISUS

A dense, bushy plant with rush-like twigs, *Cytisus × praecox* is a hybrid with the best qualities of its parents: compact growth – many cytisus tend to get leggy – and a profusion of fragrant, vivid yellow flowers in early summer. Cytisus, or brooms, are best grown on dry, sunny banks, in almost any soil, the poorer the better. They are suitable for windy sites, if staked until established. Brooms are short-lived plants, often not making ten years old, but are fast-growing, to 2–2.5m, so are easily replaced. Shear them over after flowering to encourage more compact growth. Hybrids of the yellow-flowered common broom, *C. scoparius*, often have brightly coloured keels to the flowers; look for *C.* 'Goldfinch' in red and yellow, or 'Windlesham Ruby' (*see p.10*) with slightly later flowers of ruby red. *C. × kewensis* ♀ and *C. × beanii* ♀ are excellent prostrate brooms.

CYTISUS × PRAECOX 'ALLGOLD' ♀

HELIANTHEMUM

Forming low evergreen mounds only a few centimetres high but 1m or more across, these lovely shrubs have small leaves and in early summer are covered in small, cup-shaped flowers in almost every colour except purple and blue, with yellow stamens. Closely related to cistus (*facing page*) and also known as rock roses, helianthemums enjoy the same conditions: full sun and any well-drained soil, including chalk. Pruning should be unnecessary, but they may be lightly trimmed, removing old flowerheads, afer flowering. 'Wisley Pink' (*below*) and 'Wisley Primrose' ♀, with lovely pale yellow flowers, are both especially beautiful due to their grey foliage. Other hybrids have green foliage and brightly coloured flowers: for example 'Ben Hope', carmine and deep orange, 'Amy Baring', deep buttercup-yellow, and 'Mrs C.W. Earle' ♀, bright red.

HELIANTHEMUM 'WISLEY PINK' ♀

LAVATERA

The shrubby lavateras are upright plants, 1.5–2m tall, with stiff stems and sage green leaves, flowering, usually in pinks and purples, from mid-summer until autumn. Although short-lived and not fully hardy, they grow fast and are easily grown on any well-drained to dry soil, even quite poor ground. They are also excellent in maritime areas, resisting salt winds; they need staking well, however, in exposed positions. In cold winters they may be cut down by hard frost, but can be pruned right down to the new emerging shoots at the base in early spring. Hard pruning also encourages tall, vigorous stems. 'Barnsley' ♀ (*below*), with light pink cup-shaped flowers with a dark eye, is a sport from *L. olbia*, a good shrub in its own right, as is dark pink 'Rosea'. The even darker purple-pink 'Burgundy Wine' ♀ is among the many new lavateras available.

LAVATERA 'BARNSLEY' ♀

PEROVSKIA

Perovskia atriplicifolia is an upright, greyish-white-stemmed shrub, 1–1.5m tall, with spires of lavender-blue flowers throughout late summer. The deeply cut leaves are strongly aromatic. In mild areas it will form a woody framework but in cold areas, even though it is very hardy, the top growth tends to get cut down by frosts. You can cut all the stems down hard to new emerging shoots within 15–20cm of the ground in the spring. Easily grown in full sun in any well-drained soil, perovskias tolerate very dry conditions and exposure to salt winds. Their grey and blue colouring blends perfectly with other grey-leaved plants, late summer perennials and ornamental grasses. **'Blue Spire'** ♥ (*below*) and the similar **'Superba'** are beautiful hybrids, as is **'Filigran'**, with especially finely cut leaves. *P. abrotanoides* is similar but with hairier stems.

PHLOMIS

Phlomis fruticosa ♥ is a small, rounded evergreen shrub with woolly grey-green leaves and in summer, tall stems of tiered clusters of yellow flowers, followed by attractive seedheads. It is reasonably hardy, and perfect for blending with shrubs of a similar habit and colouring such as santolinas. Known as Jerusalem sage, it will grow to about 1.25m tall in any well-drained soil in full sun, tolerating coastal and very dry conditions. Some dislike the yellow flower colour; pruning hard in early spring will ensure a mound of foliage and only a few flowers. It is advisable to prune a little every year to maintain a good shape. *P.* **'Edward Bowles'** has more attractive, paler yellow flowers. Other species include *P. chrysophylla* ♥, similar to *P. fruticosa* but with yellow-tinted leaves. *P. italica* is smaller with narrow leaves and pinky-lilac whorled flowers; it is a little less hardy.

ROSMARINUS

Rosemary (*R. officinalis, below*) is an upright evergreen, to 2m tall, that sprawls with age. It has narrow grey-green leaves that are strongly aromatic; it is a popular culinary herb. Small, pale blue flowers stud the stems in spring. From the Mediterranean, it thrives in any well-drained soil in full sun. In very cold regions it is best grown in a pot and brought indoors for winter (*see p.76*). In milder areas it can be grown as an informal hedge that can be lightly sheared after flowering. In ideal conditions it may grow up to 2m tall, but even **'Miss Jessopp's Upright'** ♥ (*see p.24*), one of the most suitable for hedging, tends to splay out unless pruned to maintain its habit. Other, prostrate types are good over stone retaining walls. **'Severn Sea'** ♥ is low-growing, more tender but with brighter blue flowers in summer. There are also rosemaries with white and pink flowers.

PEROVSKIA 'BLUE SPIRE' ♥

PHLOMIS FRUTICOSA ♥

ROSMARINUS OFFICINALIS

SANTOLINA

Santolina pinnata (*below*) is the best cotton lavender for flowers, a small evergreen shrub about 75cm tall with aromatic, feathery grey-green foliage and, in summer, many small round flowerheads on slender stalks standing up above the foliage. The flowers are a pleasing pale creamy yellow, or creamy white in '**Edward Bowles**', or primrose yellow in '**Sulphurea**'. Best grown in full sun in well-drained soils, they become leggy on soil that is too fertile. Santolinas are popular as edging for beds and herb gardens, but unfortunately flowering tends to destroy the rounded shape and dead patches often develop. Clip off the faded flowers immediately, or grow hardier *S. chamaecyparissus* ♀ as a foliage plant, pruning hard in spring to prevent flowers forming and keep the plant compact; some consider losing the brassy yellow flowers a positive advantage.

SANTOLINA PINNATA
'SULPHUREA'

YUCCA

Yuccas are dramatic evergreens with stout, sword-like leaves that stand stiffly around a woody crown, or arch over in *Y. recurvifolia* ♀ (*see p.18*). Yuccas are wonderful architectural plants as specimens or focal points in a border, or where a sub-tropical effect is wanted. The leaves of *Y. filamentosa* ♀ (*below*) are grey-green, edged with fine hairs. After about four years, a new crown will produce a magnificent spire of fragrant creamy white bells standing up to 2m high. It is easily grown in any well-drained soil in a hot position in full sun. Once established can easily withstand drought. Native to S.E. United States, it is hardy in all but the coldest regions, but dislikes winter wet. *Y. flaccida*, with leaves that bend over at the tips, is also reasonably hardy. '**Ivory**' ♀ is a good flowerer; '**Golden Sword**' ♀ is smaller, with excellent variegation. *Y. gloriosa* ♀ is a larger plant.

YUCCA FILAMENTOSA ♀

MORE CHOICES

Azara (*see p.62*)
Amelanchier canadensis (*see p.66*)
Berberis (*see pp.46, 66*)
Callistemon (*see p.62*)
Calluna (*see p.56*)
Colutea (*see p.67*)
Coronilla (*see p.63*)
Cotoneaster (*see pp.56, 60*)
Erica (*see p.56*)
Escallonia (*see p.48*)
Fremontodendron (*see p.63*)
Genista (*see p.67*)
Hippophae (*see p.68*)
Indigofera (*see p.42*)
Kerria (*see p.42*)
Pieris (*see p.59*)

Convolvulus cneorum ♀
A small, sun-loving semi-hardy shrub, to 60cm tall, with narrow leaves that have a silvery, silky sheen. Throughout the summer and into autumn, it is covered with a succession of trumpet-shaped white flowers, pink in bud and with a slight yellow throat. It requires well-drained soil, and is ideal for the front of a hot border in association with other Mediterranean shrubs such as lavender and rosemary. It can also be grown in a container, given protection in winter where necessary. It naturally forms a very neat, mounded shape and no pruning should be required.

SHRUBS FOR CONTAINERS

ABUTILON 'KENTISH BELLE' ♥
Abutilons do well in pots, in a fertile compost in full sun. In cool climates they can be overwintered in an unheated greenhouse, or may continue to flower in a conservatory. Use canes to give support.

BERBERIS × STENOPHYLLA 'CORALLINA COMPACTA' ♥
A dwarf evergreen berberis, rounded and spiny with clusters of small yellow flowers in spring. In winter, shelter from cold winds and make sure that the compost does not get waterlogged.

CALLUNA VULGARIS 'SILVER QUEEN' ♥
A lovely heather for a tub or windowbox, with silver-grey foliage all year round and pink flowers in late summer. Callunas are ideal container plants, given lime-free (ericaceous) compost.

CYTISUS × BEANII ♥
A low growing, spreading deciduous shrub that will tumble over the edges of low tubs, bearing yellow flowers in early spring. Add grit to its compost and place in full sun. Drought-tolerant, it survives some neglect in summer.

ELAEAGNUS ANGUSTIFOLIA
A beautiful medium-sized deciduous shrub with silver leaves and small, sweetly scented greenish-yellow flowers in spring. Best for full sun or partial shade. Tolerates pruning to shape.

ERICA × DARLEYENSIS 'JENNY PORTER' ♥
Evergreen, winter-flowering heathers are ideal for year-round displays. They need ericaceous compost and look good as underplanting for larger acid soil-loving shrubs such as pieris or azaleas.

CAMELLIA SASANQUA 'NARUMIGATA' ♛

Very elegant, spreading, medium-sized evergreen, with small, glossy leaves and single, pink-tinged white flowers carried in late winter and early spring. Must be grown in ericaceous compost and kept moist at all times. Good for shade. Protect from cold, drying winds.

CHOISYA TERNATA ♛

Handsome in a town garden, naturally forming a compact, rounded mound of glossy, lobed foliage (*see also p.47*) with small, white flowers in spring. In cold areas, shelter in winter. Give it a good-sized tub, in sun or shade, and feed well to maintain healthy foliage. 'Sundance' ♛ has brighter, yellow-toned leaves.

CISTUS × DANSEREAUI 'DECUMBENS' ♛

Being drought-tolerant, rock roses are splendid container shrubs. Mix some grit into the compost to give them good drainage, and shelter in winter from hard frosts and cold winds. Do not prune; if they start to look leggy, they are better planted out in the garden or replaced.

FUCHSIA 'RICCARTONII' ♛

Hardy fuchsias, unlike the showier frost-tender ones, can be left in pots outdoors all year except in very cold gardens. In spring, prune plants cut down by frost to within 10cm of the compost. Best in full sun.

HEBE ALBICANS ♛

An evergreen grey leaved hebe with white flowers in summer, forming a neat mound that suits the formal style. Use a gritty compost for good drainage, and site in full sun. Shelter in winter from cold winds and heavy frosts.

HIBISCUS ROSA-SINENSIS

A tub that can be moved into a greenhouse or conservatory over winter makes it possible to grow more tender hibiscus in cool climates. *H. rosa-sinensis* flowers all summer, in white, shades of pink, reds, oranges and yellows.

HYDRANGEA MACROPHYLLA 'LANARTH WHITE' ♀

Mophead hydrangeas make ideal container plants for sun or shade, flowering in late summer. Blue flowers can be kept blue in ericaceous compost. Prune the stems down to fat new buds in spring to keep them compact.

LAVANDULA STOECHAS ♀

Lavenders make good container plants but may be short-lived. Best grown in full sun, with some grit mixed into their compost, but do not let them dry out. In cool climates, move this French lavender under glass for protection over winter.

PIERIS JAPONICA 'PURITY' ♀

An ideal small pieris for tubs, evergreen, with sprays of white flowers in early spring. 'Little Heath' is even smaller, and will fit in a windowbox. Pieris need ericaceous compost and a fair amount of moisture, especially when in fresh growth in spring.

ROSMARINUS OFFICINALIS PROSTRATUS GROUP ♀

A creeping rosemary only 15cm tall that needs winter shelter in cold climates, but will be happy on a cool windowsill and provide sprigs for cooking. Mix some grit into its compost, and keep it in a sunny position.

SENECIO CINERARIA 'SILVER DUST' ♀

A beautiful and useful foliage plant for container displays, whose grey-yellow flowers are often trimmed off. It will not survive cold winters, but is often replaced annually: small inexpensive plants bought in spring grow away quickly.

SKIMMIA JAPONICA SUBSP. REEVESIANA

Unlike other skimmias, this flowers and fruits freely when grown on its own. Fully hardy, it does best in shade, forming a neat rounded shape. Its leaf colour is best when grown in ericaceous (lime-free) compost.

POTENTILLA FRUTICOSA 'PRIMROSE BEAUTY' ♛

Potentilla fruticosa types are among the hardiest and most easily grown deciduous shrubs for containers, flowering freely through summer. They can be trimmed over with shears in late winter to keep a neat habit. Suit full sun or partial shade.

RHODODENDRON 'VUYK'S ROSYRED' ♛

Dwarf rhododendrons and azaleas have fibrous, rather than thick, tree-like roots that make them perfect for pot-growing. Plant in ericaceous compost in full sun or shade, and keep well fed and watered throughout the year. Deadhead for more flowers.

MORE CHOICES

Convolvulus cneorum ♛ (*see p.73*)
Hypericum (*see p.49*)
Lavatera (*see p.71*)
Nandina domestica ♛ (*see p.45*)
Prunus triloba, P. tenella 'Fire Hill' ♛ (*see p.43*)
Spiraea japonica (*see p.44*)

More good camellias for containers include:

C. japonica (*see p.46*):
  'Akashigata' ♛ Deep pink
  'Debutante' Light pink
  'Guilio Nuccio' ♛ Coral
  'Lady Vansittart' White striped rose-pink
  'Masayoshi' ♛ Red petals with white marbling
  'Nobilissima' White
C. × williamsii (*see p.64*):
  'Donation' ♛ Superbly long-flowering, pink
  'Francis Hanger' White
  'Golden Spangles' Pink, leaves marked yellow

SYRINGA MEYERI 'PALIBIN' ♛

This little lilac will grow no taller than 1.2–1.5m, ideal for a tub. It has small leaves and is covered in clusters of purple-pink flowers in summer. Remove spent flower heads to encourage more flowers later in the summer.

VIBURNUM OPULUS 'COMPACTUM' ♛

A dwarf, deciduous viburnum, with clusters of white flowers followed by red berries that are popular with birds. In the autumn the leaves make a good show. A very easy and hardy plant to grow in an exposed position.

Other good rhododendrons and azaleas for containers:

• The *R. yakushimanum* hybrids named after the Seven Dwarves, e.g. 'Doc' ♛
• Dwarf evergreens:
  'Carmen' ♛ Red
  'Cilipinense' ♛ White, deep pink in bud
  'Dormouse' Pink
  Moonstone Group ♛ Cream
  'Temple Belle' ♛ Pink
  'Yellow Hammer' ♛ Yellow
• Evergreen azaleas:
  'Addy Wery' ♛ Deep red
  'Apple Blossom' Pink
  'Blaauw's Pink' ♛ Pink
  'Blue Danube' ♛ Violet
  'Hinode-giri' ♛ One of the most popular reds
  'Hinomayo' ♛ Strong red
  'Hatsugiri' ♛ Crimson
  'Mother's Day' ♛ Rose-red
  'Palestrina' ♛ White with a faint pink eye
  'Rosebud' ♛ Double pink
  'Salmon Beauty' Coral

INDEX

ACKNOWLEDGMENTS

Picture research Louise Thomas
Illustrations Karen Cochrane
Index Hilary Bird

Dorling Kindersley would like to thank:
All staff at the RHS, in particular Susanne
Mitchell, Karen Wilson and Barbara Haynes
at Vincent Square; Candida Frith-Macdonald
for editorial assistance.

Photography
The publisher would like to thank the
following for their kind permission to
reproduce their photographs:
(key: a=above; b=below; c=centre; l=left;
r=right; t=top)

Garden Picture Library: Didier Willery 66bl;
Howard Rice front cover br, back cover bl, 6,
8tr, 8b, 10bl, 11br, 19br, 38c; John Glover
17cl, 20br; J.S. Sira 9br, 77tr; Lynne Brotchie
13tr; Mayer/Le Scanff 9tl; Neil Holmes 39bl,
70bl, 72bl; Ron Evans 21tl

Garden Matters: 10br, 16br, 25tl, 76tc;
J. Feltwell 57br; John & Irene Palmer 17t,
49br; Martin P. Land 66bc; Steffie Shields
10bc
John Glover: 12tr, 18br, 22br
Jerry Harpur: 2c
Andrew Lawson: 12bl, 14bl
S & O Mathews Photography: 19t
Howard Rice: 14br, 26c
Harry Smith Collection: front cover cla,
47bc
Elizabeth Whiting & Associates:
back cover ca
Jo Whitworth: 11tl, 15tl, 15br, 23tl, 23br,
24bl, 59bl

The Royal Horticultural Society
To learn more about the work of the
Society, visit the RHS on the Internet at
www.rhs.org.uk. Information includes news of
events around the country, a horticultural
database, international plant registers, results
of plant trials and membership details.